you&your

Mazda
MX-5/Miata

you & your
Mazda
MX-5/Miata

Liz Turner

Buying, enjoying, maintaining, modifying

L133 TJK

British Library cataloguing-in-publication data:
A catalogue record for this book is available
from the British Library

Published by Haynes Publishing,
Sparkford, Yeovil, Somerset BA22 7JJ, UK

Tel: 01963 442030 Fax 01963 440001
Int. tel: +44 1963 442030 Int. fax +44 1963 440001
E-mail: sales@haynes-manuals.co.uk
Web site: www.haynes.co.uk

ISBN 1 85960 847 7

Library of Congress catalog card no. 2002107495

Haynes North America, Inc.,
861 Lawrence Drive, Newbury Park,
California 91320, USA

Printed and bound in Great Britain by
J. H. Haynes & Co. Ltd, Sparkford

Contents

Acknowledgements

This book would not have been possible without the help and support of so many people. It was a joy talking to all those involved with bringing the MX-5 into the world. Not only were their stories fascinating and sometimes very funny, but they are all still brimming over with enthusiasm for their creation.

Thanks must go first to Steve Kubo who got up at the crack of dawn in Japan to talk to me at 'Cinderella Coach time' in the UK, and who then painstakingly translated Mr Hirai's fishbone chart (page 21). I believe it is the first time it has been seen by the public, and I owe a debt of gratitude to Toshihiko Hirai for allowing me to publish his private notes.

I would also like to say thank you to Bob Hall, Mark Jordan, Norman Garrett III, Tom Matano and Peter Birtwhistle for all their time and for some great stories. I enjoyed talking to all of you.

The MX-5 is certainly unusual in having an owner's club before it was even launched, and again, I could not have written this book without the help of the clubs worldwide. I've spent many hours reading about road trips, barbies and parties, looking at photos of beautiful cars and of people in some very strange outfits. In particular, however, I'd like to thank all those club members who gave up their time to talk about MX-5s, to come on photo shoots, or who entrusted me with their precious photos and brochures. These include, in the UK, Clive and Maureen Southern, Charlotte and Doug Nadin, Andrew Fearon, Andrew Priest, Sue Duncan, John and Vanessa Batup, Colin and Hilary Frewer and Mike Hayward; Mike Hicks and Roger Tretheway in the US, and Howard Fox in New Zealand.

In particular I'd like to thank Allan Legg, Chairman of the UK Club, and his wife Joy, who came out with James Mann and I to take photos, even though they were about to become grandparents. The good news, arriving just as we had a cup of tea, put the cherry on the top of a very successful day.

I'd also like to thank Norman Garrett III, Richard Ducommun of Maztek, Keith Tanner of Flyin' Miata, and Dominic Bovington and Iain McMillan of Moss Europe for their help with the 'Mods and accessories' chapter. Richard's gorgeous supercharged MX-5 can be seen on pages 132–33, and I can testify that the acceleration forces it generates are like a brick to the head.

For the stunning pictures and information in the motorsport chapters, thanks go to Luca Pregliasco of Astra Racing in Italy, Jeff Bloxham, Alan Muir, Richard Foster, Jonathan McCormack, Danielle D. Engstrom (National Solo Communications Director for the SCCA) in the States, Darren Hodgson of DH Photo in Australia and Patrick Watts, winner of the UK one-marque championship.

For the specially commissioned photos throughout the book, I'd like to thank photographers James Mann, Dougie Firth, and Simon Farnhell. Finding the rest of the archive photos was quite a job, and I'm eternally grateful to Denni Elliot of Mazda UK, Ken Haruki, Yukari Hara, Yayoi Miyo and Furukawa Midori of Mazda Japan, Barbara Beach, publisher of *Miata Magazine* in the USA, Mark Fryer of MCL, Sue Loy and Nigel Fryatt, Mick Walsh, editor of *Classic & Sportscar*, Nigel Swan, picture editor of *What Car?*, and the ever-friendly and helpful staff at LAT.

Liz Turner
August 2002

Introduction

Driving enthusiasts all over the world should fall down on their knees and thank Mazda for the MX-5. If this cute, simple and brilliant roadster had not proved that there is a demand for a small, affordable sports car – and that there is a profit to be made from making one – there would probably be no MGF, BMW Z3, Fiat Barchetta or even Audi TT.

Back in the 1970s, in the years of BM-X ('before MX-5') the roadster was almost dead. The once teeming ranks had all but disappeared. The fear of ferocious

safety regulations being introduced in the USA killed off all but the more expensive sports models, and new cars that might have been open-tops in previous times, now sprouted metal rooflines.

By the end of the 1960s, Triumph and MG had ended up as part of the same company, BMC, and Donald

The MX-5 was, quite literally, the car enthusiasts had been waiting for; the surprise was that it wore a Japanese badge. It was, however, international teamwork that made the dream a reality. (LAT)

(later Lord) Stokes found himself in charge of a host of scattered, run-down factories and very little investment cash.

Based on the fact that the combined sales of the Triumph GT6 and TR6 had exceeded that of the MGB and MGB GT in 1968, it was decided that the next sports car would be a Triumph (even though MGBs had outsold Triumphs from 1964 to '67).

Given the flares, fat ties and triangular side-burns fashionable types chose to wear in the Seventies, the awkward wedge of cheese known as the TR7 can perhaps be forgiven, but enthusiasts still yearned for the sheer abandoned joy of a roadster. That is perhaps the only explanation of the existence of the continued sales of the Alfa Romeo Spider in 1988, which had been launched as the Duetto back in 1966.

Other choices for the enthusiast included the thrilling but thuggish TVR S with its attendant build-quality problems, and also in the UK, the underrated, sharp-handling Reliant Scimitar 1800 Ti which went like the shine off a shovel thanks to its turbocharged Nissan engine, but looked like a mouse and used Mini Metro instruments.

By the early 1980s, car magazines were constantly running wistful little pieces about the MGB replacement. (The MGF, of course, arrived about a decade late.) Nevertheless, despite the obvious gap in the market, Mazda's decision to build the MX-5 can still only be described as brave.

In 1982, Ford US produced the two-seater Barchetta concept, designed by Ghia, which was received with delight at the Frankfurt Motor Show. The numbskulls who attended subsequent focus groups, however, panned its curvy body and diminutive size, so it was put on ice and, instead, six years later, Ford offered the American public the Mercury Capri.

To western enthusiasts, with their gaze fixed on MG and Lotus, it was almost impertinent of a Japanese company to try to fill the space left by the great Brits, and beat the Italians at their own game.

In fact, the MX-5 would be one of a clutch of cars to turn the image of Japanese cars upside-down, along with the Toyota MR2 and the stunning Honda NSX, the Lexus LS400 and Nissan 300ZX, which all burst on to the scene at the end of the 1980s.

However, they were all battling against the early reputation of Japanese cars for rust, gauche looks and the liberal use of Eezee-bend metal trim. Even when their reputation for reliability and generous equipment had been laid down, Japanese cars were still easily dismissed in the West for their poor ride, uninspiring handling and characterless grey plastic interiors.

In the States, in the early 1980s, the prejudice ran deeper. Japanese imports were kicking the corporate butts in Detroit and were now officially suspected of wearing 666 badges on their boots. There were also plenty of parents and grandparents of potential buyers who still hadn't come to terms with what had happened at Pearl Harbor.

It is therefore amazing – and gratifying – that a group of like-minded and determined individuals from Japan and America, with some inspiration and help from their allies in Britain, worked together to create a car that has captured hearts all around the world.

For this, they should be congratulated, and we should give thanks again for a company brave enough to give people, not what they think they need, but what they really, really want.

Chapter **One**

East meets West Coast

From the privileged position of retrospect, it seems obvious the Mazda MX-5 had to happen – of course there would be a market for a gorgeous, inexpensive sports car. The man who actually said this out loud to Mazda's MD, Kenichi Yamamoto in 1979, US journalist Bob Hall, says now 'I'm no genius. The concept was a no-brainer. My biggest fear when we were working on the project was that someone else would do it first.'

However, no one did, and the seed Bob planted struggled like grass breaking its way through concrete before it finally saw daylight. Project chief Toshihiko Hirai has said: 'There were times when a small breeze

from the wrong direction could have blown the project away.'

His right-hand man, Steve Kubo, adds: 'There was a lot of controversy inside Mazda, because many people did not understand the necessity of an LWS (lightweight sports car). They'd say: "But we have a lot of rain! It's cold! Room for just two people? But we have a family!"

Design manager Tom Matano, says: 'When we were

Driving the dream: sun out, roof down and an open road. In the early 1980s the golden era of the roadster seemed over forever. (LAT)

working on the initial concept and a theme, we felt that it was the right car that everyone had forgotten or abandoned due to safety and other regulatory reasons. We had a conviction. I found out later that MG and others had tried to bring them back without any success. Their proposals were killed on the basis of the scale of economy at many companies. I felt that we were so fortunate because we took a very narrow window of an opportunity at the right time with the right people. In retrospect, we couldn't have done it if one of the key people was not there, or we had tried at any other time.'

Bob Hall is more blunt, saying: 'This was not a well-liked project – there were those in the company who thought it was an utter waste of money. In fact, we had to avoid some people deliberately.'

Mazda looks West

As with so many of life's pleasures, timing was everything. Mazda had suffered greatly through the oil crisis of the 1970s, but good times were on their way. We may laugh or blush (depending on our age) at the

Design genius Tsutomu 'Tom' Matano worked in Germany and Australia before joining the California team. (Mazda)

memory of designer stubble, red braces and jackets with pushed-up sleeves, but the early 1980s was an economic boom time, and Mazda was forging an astonishing recovery. Its mainstays were the 323, 626, 929 and small commercial vehicles, plus the RX-7 sports car which was selling well.

Layout engineer Norman Garrett says: 'I really don't think there was another company in the world that could have done this, who had the money, the engineering arrogance – and I mean that in a good way – who still used rear-wheel drive and happened to have a sports car which needed an entry-level smaller brother.'

The company's R&D budget at this time was bigger than that of Porsche, Mercedes and BMW combined, and since 70 per cent of its sales were in the US, the company decided to open design studios in America and Europe, to draw in some local talent and create cars to suit that market. The European office was established in Frankfurt; Mazda Automotive North America's Product Planning and Research Division, managed by Shigenori Fukuda, was founded in Irvine, California, opening fully in 1983.

The talent gathered there by the mid-1980s was astonishing. The design team brought with them experience and ideas from around the world. The supremely talented senior designer, Mark Jordan, was lured away from GM where his father Charles 'Chuck' Jordan, was vice president of design. He was working for GM's German arm, Opel, in wet, cold northern Europe, at the time so the decision to go to sunny California may not have been too hard. He was then joined by two more Opel men, Wu-Huang Chin and Matsao Yagi, with whom he'd established an excellent working relationship in Germany.

Another hero from the MX-5 hall of fame, Tsutomu (Tom) Matano, joined as manager of the design department at the end of 1983. Matano had worked in Germany for BMW and in Australia with GM-Holden as well as in Japan. His main inspirations from his days as a junior designer had been the Italian designers Giugiaro, Bertone and Pininfarina. He says: 'Today, I would add a few more people to my list. I admire Bill Mitchell [GM in the 1950s and '60s] and Tom Gayle [vice-president of design at Chrysler who directed the Viper programme and a number of show cars] both for their design and organisational leadership.'

Jordan also puts the Italians, Giugiaro and Pininfarina, on his list of inspiring designers, and adds Jean and Ettore Bugatti and French cars from the 1930s until the modern day. He says: 'Inspiration can come from anywhere: architecture, products, organic forms, but most of all I look for an energy in something and try to translate that energy into a project. When I visit somewhere like the Pebble Beach Concours, I feel a passion and energy from the artistic expression of these historic cars.'

Norman Garrett III, who went on to found the Miata Owner's Club and write the extremely readable *Mazda Miata Performance Handbook*, joined the team in 1984 as layout engineer. He describes the international team he found as: 'a bunch of hot rodders who owned 76 different sports cars between them, ranging from Austin-Healey Frogeye (or Bugeye in the USA) Sprites to Lamborghini Countachs.'

And they were based in the land not only of Deuce Coupés and lead-sleds, surf boards and movie stars but of dreams: California, with blue skies above, and the best test road in the world just outside the door, Highway One, the Pacific Coast Highway.

Bob Hall makes a suggestion

One of the first people to join the team was Bob Hall. When he arrived, however, he had no official title or a brief, and wasn't really sure what he was doing there.

He says: 'I thought I'd be in PR, but no, when I arrived I found myself in product development.'

Hall is best known worldwide as a journalist and author who has worked for prestigious car titles in the USA and Australia. He has no formal engineering qualifications, but probably inherited some gasolene in his veins from his father, who owned around 300 classic cars including British sports cars. In fact, he learned to drive in a 1955 Austin-Healey 150. ('A nice tractor with a walnut-grain dash.')

However, he went to high school in Japan, and can speak the language well enough to converse with Sydney restauranteurs and Japanese engineers alike. He says: 'I usually go back to Japan about twice a year to see friends. When I became a journalist, I built up quite a rapport with Kenichi Yamamoto and used to pop in to see him.'

One reason Hall gained favour at Mazda was that he was excited about the RX-7's Wankel rotary engine, rather than predicting its demise as an unreliable white elephant, like most of the scribblers at the time. Yamamoto would even occasionally run ideas for the

Bob Hall's hurried sketch of 1979 planted a seed in Mr Yamamoto's mind. (Mazda)

DID YOU KNOW?

Cultural differences

When the Japanese were researching what Americans wanted from a convertible, one frequent reply puzzled them. 'A lot of people said they wanted freedom' says Steve Kubo. 'In Japan the word always has a political meaning. So we were, wondering how exactly this car would improve human rights. Eventually I understood. It means freedom from daily life, duty, schedules, freedom at the weekend after all week at work.'

Shinzo 'Steve' Kubo, was MX-5 project chief Toshihiko Hirai's right-hand man. (Mazda)

RX-7 past Hall and, although any journalist would be itching to publish, Bob never betrayed his trust.

In 1979, he was West Coast editor of *Automotive News and Autoweek*, and during a now-famous conversation during his regular visit, in Spring 1979, Mr Yamamoto asked him what he thought Mazda should build next, now the RX-7 was finally on sale.

Hall says: 'The obvious idea was to build something using existing running gear. So we talked for a few minutes about what they could put together from the parts box. Then it came to me that Mazda could build a lightweight sports car based on the X508 323, because it was rear-wheel drive.'

If MG had been able to shift almost 40,000 vehicles a year during its last years, Hall was convinced a mass-produced modern and reliable equivalent could sell at least that many. He says: 'I even scribbled a quick drawing on the blackboard. But I got the impression he

wasn't very interested. That was why, when he left the room, I took a quick snap of it, because otherwise I thought I'd forget about it.'

However, Yamamoto-san didn't forget, either. In 1981, Hall found himself at MANA PP&R in California. As he says 'There I was, I wasn't a designer, I wasn't an engineer, working on design proposals.'

One of the first projects he got stuck into was the design of the tailgate for a B-series pick-up, but in February 1982, he felt a sharp tap on his shoulder and there was Mr Yamamoto. 'He asked what I was working on, and when I said a pick-up, he shook his head – they had plenty of people who could do pick-ups. He said: "That's a waste of time. You should do your sports car project."'

It was made clear that this pet project was something he should work on in his spare time, but he was joined for his Friday night homework by Mark Jordan, starting one night in March 1983. He says: 'Bob wanted me to do some sketches because he knew what he wanted to achieve, but couldn't visualise it. He started talking about the proportions and the low hood and I drew a very simple roadster with front-engined, rear-wheel-drive proportions, and it was just a little bit retro'.

LWS a-go-go

By 1983, Mr Yamamoto had been replaced as managing director by Michinori Yamanouchi who decided to set the new studios in America and Japan working on a series of stimulating offline projects, to see what they could come up with if freed from the restrictions of a production schedule. This was known as Offline Go-Go, an example of the Japanese love of English. So the project itself sounds like an echo of the 1960s.

A number of ideas were suggested, some were rejected, such as a series of modular engines and a three-wheeler, those to go ahead at MANA included an MPV, a 'kei' car (a high-tech mini car), a pick-up – and, of course, the roadster, known in the initial-crazy Mazda parlance as LWS (lightweight sports car).

The so-called Tokyo studio – actually in a rented office just outside Hiroshima – headed by Yoichi Sato, decided to make two coupés, one with a front engine and front-wheel-drive layout (FF) and a rear-wheel-drive, mid-engined model, that is the engine would be behind the driver, but ahead of the rear wheels (MR).

The FF would be popular with the company's accountants because it could possibly be based on the platform for the new 323. However, the resulting car would have faced all the criticisms levelled at the Punto-based Fiat Barchetta, that it looked great, but didn't drive like a proper roadster.

It would probably have suited less experienced or enthusiastic drivers, because front-wheel-drive cars tend to understeer. So, if you hammer too fast into a bend, the car will try to keep heading straight on rather than going round the bend. The natural reaction is to back off the throttle a bit, and then the nose tucks safely back in again.

Like the Mini, the FF concept provided a neat engineering solution because the engine runs across the engine bay (mounted transversely) and transfers its drive to the wheels either side. That means more cabin space, with no bulky transmission tunnel required to run down the centre of the car.

The disadvantage, however, is that the front wheels are trying to do two jobs at once – both putting the engine's power down to the road and steering. The result can often be a tugging sensation at the wheel, or in a more powerful car, the wheels may simply spin as you try to turn out of a junction. Considering these problems, it was a real surprise when Lotus chose this route for its new Elan (see pages 32 and 33).

The mid-engined, rear-wheel-drive structure is a classic sports car layout, which allows a perfect 50/50 weight split. It is favoured by Ferrari and Fiat's X1/9 and was very fashionable at the time, being used by several generations of the Toyota MR2. However, in practical terms, it usually means a small luggage bay at the back (or none at all in the case of the current MR2) and room for a few odds and ends under a front bonnet, sharing space with the spare wheel. Rover opted for this layout for the MGF, and an added consequence is that the MG team has still not worked out a way to fit a glass rear window. The MX-5 had one by 1998.

MANA's LWS would have a classic front-engined, rear-wheel-drive layout, still allowing a good front-to-rear balance, but also allowing each pair of wheels to get on with a single job – the rear wheels to drive the car and the front wheels to steer. This layout is recognised as a favourite for enthusiastic drivers, but in the early 1980s, it was regarded as old fashioned, and a backward step, because of the way the rear end can step out (much to the delight of those enthusiastic sideways drivers).

The three models came together at Mazda's Hiroshima HQ in 1984, the MANA model's featured a removable hard-top, seen here on the ground to the left of the car. (Mazda)

DID YOU KNOW?

What happened to IAD

IAD appeared destined for great things in the 1980s. The company had branches all over the world, including the USA and Russia. It worked on concept cars such as the futuristic Lotus Venus and the Lincoln Town car, as well as providing an essential subsidiary role for the Mazda design teams.

Tragically, its charismatic proprietor, John Shute, lost his fight with cancer, just as the MX-5 was being taken to people's hearts around the world. IAD was sold to Daewoo in 1994, and the acclaimed Matiz was produced at the Worthing studio which had created the V705 prototype for Mazda. This facility was sold to TWR in 2001.

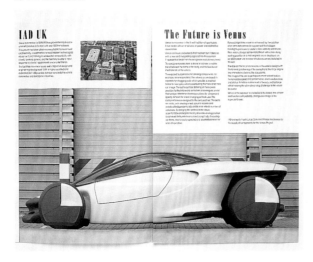

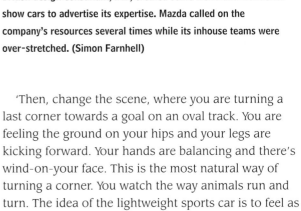

British design consultant, IAD, created some weird and wonderful show cars to advertise its expertise. Mazda called on the company's resources several times while its inhouse teams were over-stretched. (Simon Farnhell)

Tom Matano says: 'The mid-ship layout was developed for racing cars to get maximum cornering adhesion, it's designed for the track, but it feels artificial when compared to the FR (front-rear) layout.

'The lightweight sports car is like a pair of jogging shoes; the mid-ship layout is like a pair of spiked shoes. It should be better for much higher performance sports cars.

'The FF [front engine/front-wheel-drive] layout is like riding a chariot. It is not a natural movement when turning a corner.'

To describe why the LWS should be rear-wheel drive, Tom uses the example of a horse and rider – a theme that frequently recurs in the MX-5 story. He says: 'I asked everyone in the room to close their eyes to picture racehorses turning a last corner and heading for the finish line. They are kicking their hind legs to push forward, their fore legs are balancing and aiming towards the home stretch.

'Then, change the scene, where you are turning a last corner towards a goal on an oval track. You are feeling the ground on your hips and your legs are kicking forward. Your hands are balancing and there's wind-on-your face. This is the most natural way of turning a corner. You watch the way animals run and turn. The idea of the lightweight sports car is to feel as close to this natural feeling in a four-wheeled vehicle.

'I am not sure whether my racehorse won the argument or not. But, from that day onward, this engine layout issue was not discussed. It may have been a pivotal moment for the MX-5 development. Mark Jordan agrees, saying: 'A mid-engined layout would have been totally wrong.'

Three cars go head to head

The first drawings for the MANA LWS, known as P729, were produced by Jordan and Yagi. Jordan has always been a Ferrari fan, and he admits there's a touch of the prancing horse about some of his early sketches. However, he insists his strongest influence was the original Lotus Elan, saying: 'The Elan was the most ideal basis for this car.'

The first hurdle was a trip to Hiroshima in April 1984 where the two studios were to show their work. MANA's sketches were considered rather flat and Hall believes strongly that at this point, the LWS was pronounced clinically dead.

However, the Japanese management felt sorry for the American team, and did not want to crush their enthusiasm so early on with their very first project. So the team was allowed to take the project to clay model stage.

When the model arrived, however, the pendulum swung back towards the West. Sato has said: 'Maybe I was seeing a false image, or didn't see through the real value of the (first) MANA presentation. The roadster was neat and clean, but wasn't really animated. Little did I know that MANA would return with vengeance and such whack four months later.'

In September 1984, the two teams and their three models met again in Hiroshima. The Tokyo Studio's MR car was an angular vehicle which looked very similar to Toyota's recently revealed concept MR2, (the production car was launched in March 1985). They had even built a running prototype similar in concept to mid-engined performance hot hatches such as the Renault 5 Turbo 2, but ran into problems with noise, vibration and harshness (NVH) because of the firm sporty suspension. Simply softening the suspension would have spoiled the whole effect, so this option was terminated.

The front-drive version looked surprisingly similar to its mid-ships brother, although with slimmer pillars and more of a coupé slope to its roof. It wouldn't turn heads, however. Even at this stage, MANA's model had the feminine curves, pop-up headlamps, open mouth of the production car. (Although perhaps its expression was closer to one of surprise than the now-familiar lovable smile.) It was parked between the two coupés wearing a hard-top with the gaps covered over by red tape and was favourably received, but then the team whipped off the roof and brought the house down.

Bob Hall remembers: 'The leader of the other studio, Sato, leapt up and said: "We must build this!"'

MANA's roadster was a brave concept, its front-engined, rear-wheel-drive layout was considered old-fashioned. (Mazda)

At the end of session, the coupés were wheeled away to the dustbin of history, but the FR roadster was still anything but Go Go. This was an offline project, and most people at Mazda still felt there was no perceived market for it. Also, Mazda's PP&D department was swamped with projects considered to be more immediate and more important. These included the 1985 Tokyo Motor Show experimental GT, the MX-03 powered by a triple-rotor engine and featuring four-wheel drive and four-wheel steering. Then there was the idea of a 323 convertible and the MPV also developed from the offline work, with which the LWS was now competing for development cash.

IAD's prototype wows Santa Barbara

In Summer 1985, the British design agency IAD, was commissioned to build a running prototype of the LWS. At the time, IAD was a hot new, cutting-edge design company, based in Worthing in the UK, but with offices in France, Germany, Japan, Moscow and California. It turned heads at every motor show with concepts such as the swoopy Lotus-based Venus sports car, which showed only an inch or so of tyre below its four enclosed pods, or a mini-MPV, almost a decade before the Renault Mégane Scenic.

No dimensions for the car to be known as the V705 had been laid down, but the designers at IAD were given the existing clay model and sketches, plus a list of parts from Mazda's existing products. They started with MacPherson struts from a 323 and an engine from a 929 wagon, and created a vehicle similar in construction to the original Lotus Elan with a solid backbone chassis and a GRP body. The red and white interior featured a large console stretching down the centre of the cabin and a furry hand-rest on the two-spoke steering wheel.

It looked the part, but it was big and underpowered, or as Bob Hall put it: 'On a hot day it wouldn't have got out of the depressions it made in the tarmac.'

In September 1985, a number of members of the MANA team flew to Britain and tried it out at the grey, cheerless Ministry of Defence test track facility known simply to British automotive journalists as 'Chobham'. (This facility can be spotted in hundreds of UK magazine and TV shoots simply because it is a safe and convenient place for action photography. However, as

Tokyo's front-engined, front-wheel-drive coupé would have pleased the accountants, but not the enthusiasts. (Mazda)

Mark Jordan remembers, those using it have to watch out for army tanks.)

Jordan wrote in a memo: 'We conducted a test drive of the V705 with three competitor vehicles: a Fiat X1/9, a Reliant Scimitar and a Toyota MR2. We tested each car on a high-speed loop, a road course and a skid pan. The Mazda prototype was completely functional, even down to the cigarette lighter, and felt very realistic as a production model.'

Looking back he says: 'The guys at IAD did a great job, but when I look at that car now, it had the round mouth shape, but its doors and the back were so flat. Cars around us at the time were so tight and angular like the Honda CRX and the Pontiac Fiero, that that rounded shape was completely out of the industry. We needed to get that timeless roadster shape, which would live through the trends and wear well in the long-term future. That meant it might not be the trendiest and most fashionable on the block, but it would be one of the most satisfying for the long term. Our next two models became more and more rounded as we went along. That was really quite radical at the time.'

The prototype's next stop was due to be Hiroshima, but the managing director in charge of Mazda's Testing and Research Division, Masataka Matsui, decided he wanted to drive the car in its natural habitat, first. So, in October 1985, the V705 stopped off in California, escorted by John Shute, the charismatic proprietor of IAD, and Mr Matsui flew in to LA to take a test drive through Santa Barbara.

In retrospect, this was not a smart move if the company wanted to keep the project secret. Santa Barbara is full of car nuts who were not fooled by the phoney Toyota badge on the car's number plates.

Norman Garrett remembers: 'Swarms of people were chasing us. We passed a Porsche showroom with about half a dozen people in there looking at 911s, but as we stopped at the lights, one by one they came across and had their noses up against the glass looking at us.'

As if by magic, cameras appeared, and Garrett almost drove over one determined individual, but there was worse to come. As the car crawled past a café in State Street, trapped in a tight traffic jam, Bob Hall's horrified eyes met those of an astonished group of journalists and a photographer from *Road & Track*,

Mid-engined, rear-wheel-drive layout used by Tokyo's MR Coupé was popular at the time; it was used by the MR2 and, later, the MGF. (Mazda)

having lunch after a coast-to-coast drive for a feature in the magazine. Coffees and jaws were dropped, and hall had to make a frantic trip to the office to plead with the editor, John Dinkel, to stifle the scoop of the decade.

He says: 'I said, if they wanted to see a car like this built, they mustn't write about it. It would have been so easy for it to be killed off. And they didn't publish a word.'

That night, an elated group including Matsui, Garrett, Hall, Tom Matano, chief engineer Toshihiko Hirai, Steve Kubo and Shigenori Fukuda had dinner, and talked for hours over several bottles of wine. Discussions of thrilling and responsive transport lead to a session of 'horse talk' and it was probably here that Mr Hirai came up with the slogan that would hang above the studio where the MX-5 was born: 'Oneness of horse and rider'.

At the meal, the Americans were lobbying hard. Matsui had enjoyed the car and was impressed by the response to it, but he was still cautious. Were people just excited because they didn't know what the prototype was? Was it just because it was red and sporty?

'We were walking back to the hotel,' says Garrett, 'and Mr Matsui looked up at the sky and just said: "Maybe we should build this car". And all of us wanted to punch the air and cheer. If it had the support of such an influential man, it was going to happen.'

The next stage in the long, slow process was a feasibility study, and finally some proper money was put into the project. At this stage, Tom Matano was design manager, with Mark Jordan as senior designer, working with the talented Wu-Huang Chin, who would continue to work on future generations of MX-5. The clay modellers from IAD now also decamped to the California studio to work on the project, adding some razor-sharp humour to the excitement in the studio. Mark Jordan says: 'IAD had a great programme of being able to contract out their people. We had a choice of a couple of companies, but we were impressed by their talent. They were great modellers, including Martin McCreath and Brian Innocent.'

One day the latter was outside helping Bob Hall work on his MGA, and mentioned casually that he had worked on the model of the original.

A test drive was also undertaken in Japan in which a

MX-04 CONCEPT 1987

Mazda gave a tempting taste of what was to come when it unveiled the MX-04 at the 1987 Tokyo Motor Show. The MX-02 and MX-03 had both been rather uninspiring family cars, but this car was a sporty two-seater. The chassis could be fitted with a choice of three glassfibre bodies, a wedge-shaped coupé, or two different

The wedge-shaped MX-04 Coupé was shown at the 1987 Tokyo Motor Show. It had four-wheel drive and a choice of three bodies. (LAT)

roadsters, none of which shared the finished MX-5's curves.

There were major differences under the skin, too. The MX-04 was powered by a rotary engine and had electronically controlled four-wheel drive. However, it shared the backbone chassis developed for the new car and used a similar double-wishbone suspension set-up.

Suzuki displayed a mid-engined roadster concept at the same show, causing Mazda executives a few sleepless nights as they wondered whether another manufacturer might pip their LWS to the post.

convoy of lucky drivers took turns to exercise their right feet around mountain roads in a 911 Cabriolet, a Fiat X1/9, Fiat Spider 2000, a Lotus 7 and an Elan, and make notes. Typically, the Elan's shock's had gone and the electrics were playing up, but everyone agreed it was the most enjoyable and direct-feeling car. Norman Garrett comments: 'People say we copied the Elan. In fact there's not a single nut or bolt shared, but we wanted to capture its spirit.'

A second full-size model of the LWS was completed by December 1985 and a month later, serious studies into production feasibility began. It was still possible

that the next car on the MANA list would have been the kei car, which was technically innovative, but probably suitable only for the Japanese market.

Instead, Fukuda was lobbying for the LWS. He said to Yamanouchi Michinori: 'There's something about this car. Everyone working on it feels something. Surely this passion must translate to the market.'

He got his wish. The LWS was presented to the board of Mazda's managing directors and Bob Hall's old friend, Kenichi Yamamoto, now president of the company, supported the project wholeheartedly. At last, the LWS was going into production.

Chapter **Two**

Creating the perfect roadster

Once the official go-ahead had been given for the lightweight sports car, in January 1986, a project manager was appointed. Step forward Toshihiko Hirai, chief engineer and to many the father of the MX-5. (Barbara Beach, publisher of *Miata Magazine*, suggests this makes Bob Hall the biological father, while Hirai was the man who nurtured the Mazda to adulthood.)

The Japanese do not have the same history of building or driving small sports cars as the British and Americans, but Hirai understood exactly what the LWS should be and how to achieve it. Although he has now retired, members of the team still speak of him with a respect bordering on reverence.

A broad outline had already been established. The LWS should be a traditional sports car with an engine in the front and the power should be laid down by the rear wheels. The gearchange should be short and snick into place, the steering should be sharp and communicative. The engine should be a four-cylinder twin-cam; Mazda's famous rotary engine simply did not have the right personality. Marketing necessity

DID YOU KNOW?

Porsches over the limit
Mazda's engineers 'totalled' three Porsche 944s, described by *Car & Driver* at the time as 'the best handling car in the world', while examining the on-the-limit handling. They knew that some of the most exciting cars tend to swap ends when pushed, and were keen to avoid this. As at least one British journalist spun the MX-5 on the first Japanese test drive, they may have been a little disappointed, but the MX-5 is still one of the most forgiving and predictable sports cars on the market.

also dictated it should be relatively low-powered. This was partly to separate it from the RX-7, but more importantly, it was to keep insurance costs low. Having seen the Honda CRX and then a whole generation of hot hatches killed off by huge insurance premiums, this is a policy Mazda has stuck to throughout the MX-5's life. Repair costs were also high on the list when choosing parts and designing body panels, again to keep premiums low.

The new car would be close in spirit to an MG Midget or a Sprite, cheap, cheerful but great fun at the weekend and capable of taking to the track.

Mark Jordan says: 'As enthusiastic car guys, we always want more power. But the balance was so good, that it was not just about the engine power, but the overall handling and the exhilaration of the car.'

Bob Hall christened it the KISS car, as in: Keep It Simple, Stupid. And yet creating such a car was anything but simple. As well as such technical considerations as judging the inevitable compromise between flat cornering and ride comfort, performance versus economy, compact size and decent legroom, the team also had to take into consideration a raft of legislation covering emissions and crashworthiness. Then, of course, there was the high level of convenience and luxuries expected by drivers in the '90s compared with those in the glory days of the 1960s. In fact, in terms of equipment, the MX-5 would offer more electrical goodies as standard than most family models in the UK.

Mr Hirai approached this task by laying down the essentials for the LWS on what assistant Steve Kubo describes as his 'Fish skeleton' chart. Translated into English by Steve Kubo for this book, the chart has a central backbone running across the page with six lines, like ribs drawn at right angles to it.

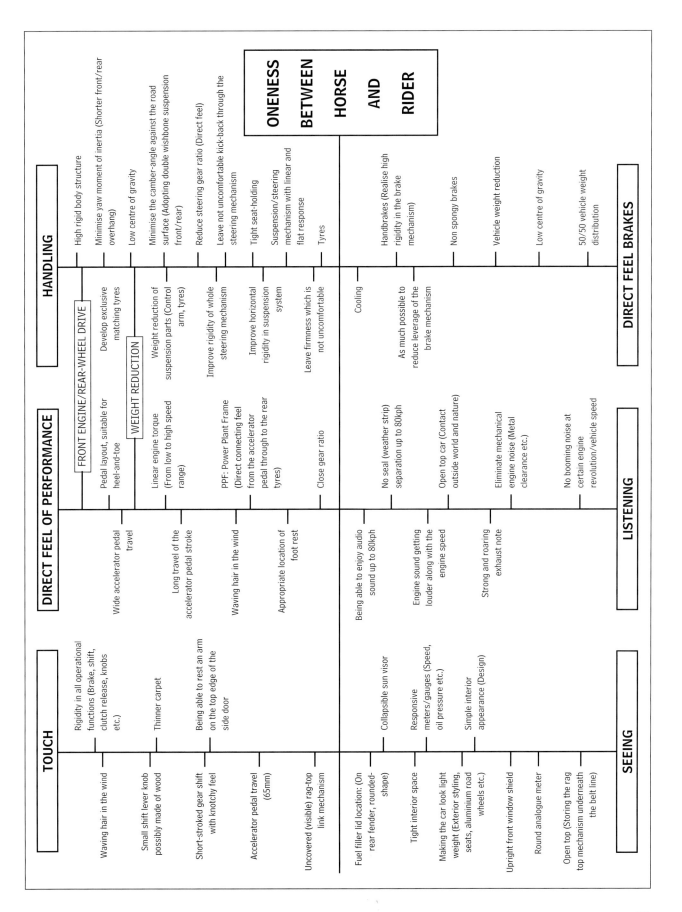

TOUCH

Waving hair in the wind — Rigidity in all operational functions (Brake, shift, clutch release, knobs etc.)

Small shift lever knob possibly made of wood — Thinner carpet

Short-stroked gear shift with knotchy feel — Being able to rest an arm on the top edge of the side door

Accelerator pedal travel (65mm) — Appropriate location of foot rest

Uncovered (visible) rag-top link mechanism

DIRECT FEEL OF PERFORMANCE

Wide accelerator pedal travel — Pedal layout, suitable for heel-and-toe

Long travel of the accelerator pedal stroke — Linear engine torque (From low to high speed range)

Waving hair in the wind — PPF: Power Plant Frame (Direct connecting feel from the accelerator pedal through to the rear tyres)

Close gear ratio

FRONT ENGINE/REAR-WHEEL DRIVE

WEIGHT REDUCTION

Develop exclusive matching tyres

Weight reduction of suspension parts (Control arm, tyres)

Improve rigidity of whole steering mechanism

Improve horizontal rigidity in suspension system

Leave firmness which is not uncomfortable

HANDLING

High rigid body structure

Minimise yaw moment of inertia (Shorter front/rear overhang)

Low centre of gravity

Minimise the camber-angle against the road surface (Adopting double wishbone suspension front/rear)

Reduce steering gear ratio (Direct feel)

Leave not uncomfortable kick-back through the steering mechanism

Tight seat-holding

Suspension/steering mechanism with linear and flat response

Tyres

LISTENING

Being able to enjoy audio sound up to 80kph — No seal (weather strip) separation up to 80kph

Engine sound getting louder along with the engine speed — Cooling

Strong and roaring exhaust note — Open top car (Contact outside world and nature)

Eliminate mechanical engine noise (Metal clearance etc.)

No booming noise at certain engine revolution/vehicle speed

As much possible to reduce leverage of the brake mechanism

DIRECT FEEL BRAKES

Handbrakes (Realise high rigidity in the brake mechanism)

Non spongy brakes

Vehicle weight reduction

Low centre of gravity

50/50 vehicle weight distribution

SEEING

Fuel filler lid location: (On rear fender, rounded-shape) — Collapsible sun visor

Tight interior space — Responsive meters/gauges (Speed, oil pressure etc.)

Making the car look light weight (Exterior styling, seats, aluminium road wheels etc.) — Simple interior appearance (Design)

Upright front window shield

Round analogue meter

Open top (Storing the rag top mechanism underneath the belt line)

ONENESS BETWEEN HORSE AND RIDER

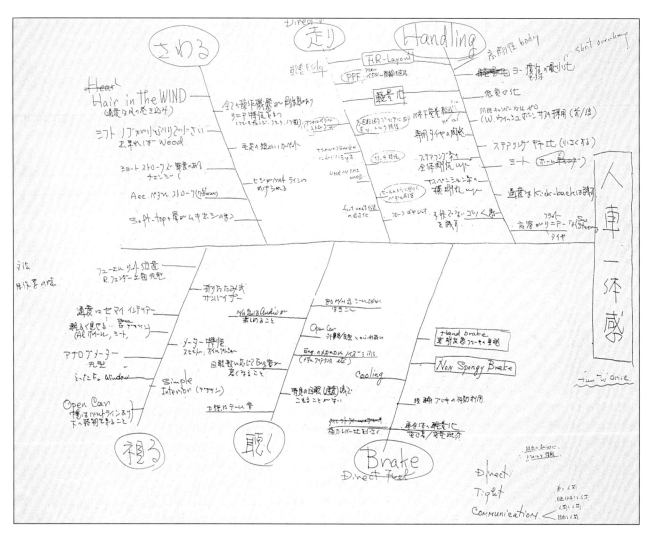

Toshihiko Hirai laid down every aspect of the LWS in this chart, and made certain that the team stuck to it. As a result, every phrase on this page describes the MX-5 perfectly. (Simon Farnhell, courtesy Mazda)

This car needed *kan sei*, which in engineering terms translates roughly as 'feel'. So the ribs are labelled 'Seeing', 'Listening', 'Touch', 'Direct feel of brakes', 'Direct feel of performance' and 'Handling', the last two being linked by horizontal lines labelled 'Front engine/Rear-wheel drive' and 'Weight reduction'. More markers with notes along each rib note how the main objective set by that line can be achieved. For example, in 'Seeing', he notes that the open top must be stored below the deck line and that the fuel filler and dials should be round. Under 'Listening', he demands a strong and roaring exhaust note, yet the driver must be able to enjoy their radio at up to 80kph (50mph). Under 'Touch', he notes that you must be able to rest an arm on the top edge of the door. Under 'Direct feel of

performance' he has added 'Waving hair in the wind'. All these things are essential to the roadster experience. It is also remarkable to realise that every note on the chart describes the MX-5 perfectly, and despite the difficulties, the team never deviated from it – even though many of them never knew it existed.

Elements noted along the more technical lines of the chart include 'Linear engine torque', 'Close gear ratios' and 'Weight reduction', including a note revealing that Mr Hirai had already decided that exclusive matching tyres would be needed to reduce unsprung weight.

At the end of the fish's backbone is the slogan which was hung above the studio: 'Oneness of horse and rider'. This phrase is known to riders all over the world and is commonly used to describe the pinnacle of achievement in dressage, but had also been used to describe the immaculate balance and trust between native Americans and their horses.

For Steve Kubo, it had a personal significance as he regularly enjoyed riding at the Serrano Creek Ranch in

California. However he says it also summoned up an image of a Samurai warrior and his horse. 'Everything is under control, he knows every move.'

Mark Jordan says: 'It was a key phrase we were to follow. We would say to ourselves that this was the type of car you wore. The feedback from any part of this car had to be beyond doubt.'

To achieve the goals on Mr Hirai's list, layout specialist Masaaki Watanabe and his team adhered to the principles so beloved by Colin Chapman: weight should be reduced, while the body should be as rigid as possible, allowing the suspension to do its job.

Engineer Norman Garrett comments: 'The Japanese are very philosophical and I think this project suited their way of thinking because we were searching for the pure essence. Like Colin Chapman, we wanted simplicity and efficiency, ideas which also fit in with the Japanese love of minimalism.'

In some ways, Mazda's lack of sports car heritage was a real advantage. It meant the team could start with a clean sheet and no preconceptions. However, the company's brilliant engineers had access to the most up-to-date technology.

Mazda was already committed to reducing the weight of all its vehicles, and had made great advances

DID YOU KNOW?

Mazda Laguna?

Mazda seriously considered calling its new sports car the Laguna, after California's Laguna Seca race track, because it was felt that this summed up the spirit of the car. However, it doesn't roll easily off the tongue. In fact, say it quickly and it sounds like a garbled Spanish greeting (Mazda Laguna, baby).

Then Mazda US product planning executive Rod Bymaster spotted the word Miata in Webster's Dictionary. Meaning 'reward' in Old High German, it sounds right, and the sentiments are perfect. Driving the Miata is a reward. The name is not used in Japan because there was already a Miyata bicycle on sale there.

in the science of building lightweight vehicles. Plus, as Watanabe's engineers worked to create a strong rigid tub, to eliminate the evils of vibration and 'scuttle shake' the MX-5 became one of the first cars to use computer modelling for the entire design process.

The IAD prototype had used GRP for the body, but

Balanced handling was to be the core value rather than power; the 1.6-litre MX-5 won *Autocar*'s handling day in July 1990. (LAT)

the real thing would be a steel structure, using aluminium and plastic where possible. One of the largest body panels on the car, the bonnet, has an aluminium skin – as many British sports cars did, including the MGA. Strength was put into the front and rear bulkheads, door sills and the floorpan.

To achieve the required feeling of directness between the throttle and rear wheels, Hirai had laid down in his chart that the car would have a power plant frame (PPF), or a torque-tube structure. This featured a rigid beam of cast aluminium, offset to one side, with the engine and gearbox assembly bolted on at one end, and the rear differential at the other, resembled the backbone chassis of the Lotus Elan. It was previously favoured by far more expensive machinery including the Ferrari Daytona, Porsche 928 and the C4 and C5 Corvettes. It reduces drivetrain wind-up and release (or shunt) as the throttle is

To create a feeling of instant response, a power plant frame (PPF) runs along the right-hand side of the propshaft connecting the engine and gearbox to the final drive assembly at the rear. (Mazda)

opened up or closed, and as a bonus, assembly line time can be reduced.

From 1992, Mazda added a rear subframe brace which reduced the infamous 65mph vibration, and made the rear subframe more resistant to deflection under cornering loads, so the wheels and tyres stay in better alignment with the ground.

In 1994, when the 1.8 engine was introduced, the front and rear subframes were stiffened and braced, greatly improving rigidity and reducing flex in the platform.

For ultimate stability and grip, the team worked very hard on simply keeping as much of the footprint of the tyre flat on the tarmac for as much of the time as possible. To do so, they opted for a suspension set-up that was well tried and well proven.

The double-wishbone with coil-over shock absorbers will also be familiar to Ferrari fans. This arrangement is a favourite for sports cars because it provides optimum camber during cornering.

Another goal on Mr Hirai's fish skeleton was natural toe-in during cornering. This creates a stable

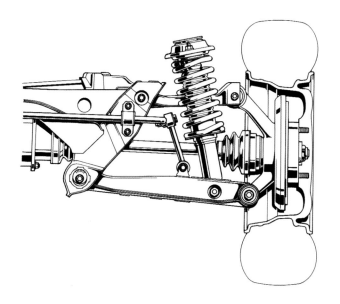

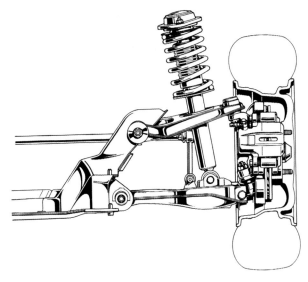

Classic double-wishbone suspension uses unequal-length upper and lower arms at both front and rear. (Mazda)

Front suspension viewed from the front; rack-and-pinion steering gear is mounted in front of the subframe. (Mazda)

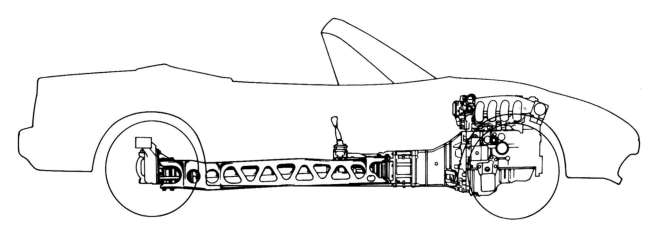

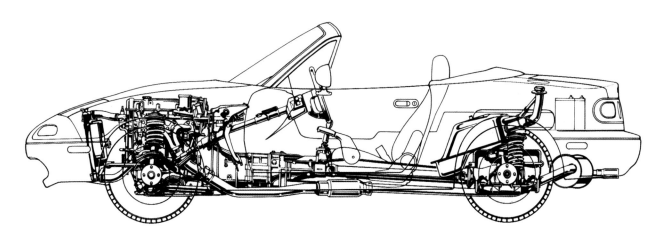

Pressed, perforated aluminium PPF was designed with the help of Mazda's sophisticated computer design programs. (Mazda)

A rigid, yet light structure was essential to the car's character; wheels and tyres were made specially to reduce the weight. (Mazda)

suspension under neutral conditions and tends to damp out the forces of both engine and brake-induced deceleration. It was accomplished by locating the upper control arm ahead of the wheel centreline, creating a torque arm when side forces are introduced.

Weight distribution was also critical to the MX-5's delicately balanced handling. To keep the car flat on the road, a low centre of gravity was essential, and to achieve neutral handling on corners, Hirai noted a 50/50 front-to-back distribution to his chart (for the Mk1 it was actually 52/48 front-to-rear unladen).

Unsprung weight, another enemy of handling, had to be reduced. To explain: springs and shock absorbers support the car's body and chassis as the car moves, but they do not support the wheel, tyres and brake assemblies, so the suspension designer must keep these 'unsprung' pieces as light as possible, allowing them to react quickly to road inputs. A heavy wheel has more inertia when it is deflected upwards by a bump than a light one, so it will lose contact with the road longer, a lightweight wheel will also jar occupants less.

Power came from Mazda's proven Type B6-ZE double-overhead camshaft 16-valve 1,597cc four-cylinder engine. It is mated to a development of Mazda's M-type five-speed transmission. (Mazda)

This explains why cost-conscious Mazda went to the expense of creating strong, but super-light, alloy wheels and commissioned special tyres from Dunlop. A press release issued at the time of the UK launch of the MX-5 in 1990 reads: 'The new lightweight Dunlop tyre allows full use to be made of the MX-5's roadholding ability and its tread pattern enhances the MX-5's elegant roadster appearance … Originally developed for use in the USA and Japan, subtle changes have been made to suit road conditions in the UK and Europe, with our need for enhanced wet grip.'

A Kevlar crossply 165/555-14in slick or treaded wet-weather form was made available for racing.

The original wheel resembles original 1960s Minilites, although it only has seven spokes as opposed to the classic eight, much to the disgust of some classic car fans. Norman Garrett claims the American team deliberately fitted the final model with a set of Panasport wheels on one side of the final model 'to give the corporate guys a hint'.

Powering up the Mk1

The engine began life as the 1.6-litre four-cylinder unit also used by the Mazda 323, with a cast-iron block and twin camshafts driving 16 valves. But before it settled

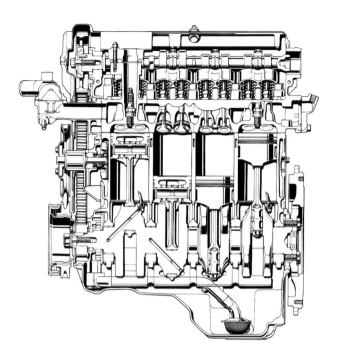

beneath the MX's bonnet it was lovingly hot-rodded by the same brilliant engineers who had massaged the Wankel rotary engine into reliable life. The compression ratio was raised to 9.4:1 to increase power across the rev range. The cylinder head was ported for optimum horsepower and torque, and the camshafts were reshaped to maximise flow at high rpm. Precise amounts of fuel were delivered by a Multipoint fuel injection system. The crankshaft, rods and pistons were lightened to improve throttle response. A windage tray was added to the aluminium oil sump to reduce drag on the crankshaft from foaming oil.

Power was a modest 116bhp delivered at 6,500rpm and 110lb ft of torque was delivered at a sky-high 5,500rpm, but its response from 2,000rpm was excellent. Another impressive figure, thanks to its trim waistline, was 72.5bhp per litre.

The Mk1 likes to rev hard, and the engine tuning is designed to maximise power while giving an ever-increasing sense of acceleration (as noted on Hirai's chart) to subtly give the driver the impression there's more power than is actually there.

When it came to the exhaust system, the team had two vital and equally important goals. It not only had to let the engine breath efficiently (while meeting all the modern emissions regulations) it also had to make the right, satisfying noise. Hirai's aim was to create a powerful low-frequency sound while eliminating resonance or boom and he taped his favourite exhaust notes – including those of the BMW M1 – and played them on his way to work.

In all, the team tried 25 different exhaust systems, before settling on the production stainless steel system. This has a tubular, low-restriction header (manifold), and well tuned muffler (silencer) which gives a crisp, throaty sound that tells anyone who's listening there's a sports car coming. In countries such as Japan and America, the system also featured a high-flow catalytic

Mazda's four-cylinder, inline engine produced 114bhp at 6,500rpm and 100lb ft of torque at 5,500rpm. (Mazda)

Twin overhead camshafts are driven by a single-stage cogged belt and operate four valves per cylinder via inverted bucket-type tappets. (Mazda)

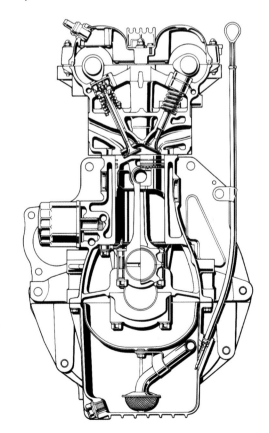

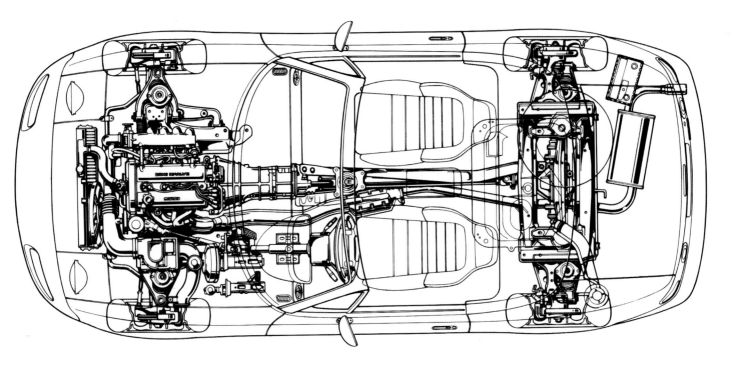

The MX-5 has a very traditional sports car layout, and to achieve its supremely balanced handling, as much weight as possible is kept within the wheelbase. (Mazda)

converter, but in the UK, this did not become standard until 1993.

The driver reaches out to grab the performance using one of the most satisfying gearchanges on the market. The lever is deliberately small and stubby, its action

Pop-up headlamps were common in the 1980s because large lamps were still necessary to achieve sufficient illumination. (LAT)

short, matched by that of the short clutch pedal which is precise and decisive. The thrill comes as the revs rise, the car shoots forward, then the lever snicks through the gate without hesitation or undue pressure, and you're off.

The steering, too, is quick and exact, feeding back exactly what the wheels are doing. Each of these actions was studied, considered and perfected long before the eager buyers got to experience the thrill of an MX-5.

Once again IAD were called in to assist by producing a series of test mules, and to help design the roof. Mr Hirai's specifications were that it had to be easily erected or stowed from the driving seat, and its latch had to be simple to use. It had to seal and keep the cabin snug and quiet at up to 80mph. Once folded, it had to stow completely below the car's rear deck line without taking up the entire boot.

The team also had to consider the comfort of those in the car when the roof was folded, but the idea of a windblocker was rejected outright (a decision which has made a lot of money for accessory suppliers like Oris). The feeling of wind rushing through the follicles was too important to the roadster experience to be blocked out entirely. So the model went into a wind tunnel with a manikin head covered in long threads of yarn to make sure there was just enough – but not too much – breeze running through its imaginary follicles.

According to Steve Kubo, the inspiration for this came mainly from old Hollywood posters and films. He says: 'A beautiful actress gets into the car and her hair blows in the wind. We wanted to have some mild "wind squall". So we took a prototype to a wind tunnel and studied the windscreen angle and the door mirrors (which have a very important effect).'

The pop-up headlamps, often assumed these days to have been a deliberately nostalgic touch, were actually forced by necessity. The new car needed good lights, and at the time, that meant a large lamp area, and the pop-up solution was used by a large number of cars at the time, from the MR2 to Porsches. By 1998, when the Mk2 was introduced, the large lamps – and therefore the pop-ups were no longer needed.

No one who has ever sat in a modern Mazda, Nissan or Toyota, would need to be told that the MX-5's interior was designed in Japan. To many owners it is the weakest area of the car, and it is a feature that has spawned an accessory market for those who want to brighten up the cheerless plastic with chrome vent rings, coloured dials and console inserts.

The seats and cabin were also clearly created using Japanese human resource data, and so Mazda drivers tend to be under six-foot tall. Large bottoms don't fit easily, either.

It constantly surprises this author that the Japanese have such a clear appreciation of textures when it comes to silk, water and stone, but somehow this never translates into the plastic surfaces within a car.

Mazda describes the interior as simple, like the Japanese tea ceremony. A more widely held opinion is that it's plain and rather disappointing, given the beauty of the exterior. (Mazda)

Shunji Tanaka refined the lines of the original Mk1, much to the distress of the American team. (Mazda)

Tanaka was inspired by laquered Noh masks, which change expression as they are tilted in the light. (Embassy of Japan)

Tom Matano agrees that the interior is simple, and feels that part of the appeal of the Mazda is the opportunity to personalise it, as so many owners have done.

Mark Jordan comments 'Perhaps it is too plain; it didn't have the character it could have done. It would have benefited from a couple more inches of legroom, too.'

Hiroshima has the final word

Any project involving real passion is also guaranteed to see frayed nerves, bruised egos and hear plenty of raised voices. Despite the harmony of the MX-5's design, at times the atmosphere in the design and engineering studios was far from tranquil.

There were personality clashes, culture clashes and language barriers. Mr Hirai was often the arbiter, but in turn, he fought with Mr Tachibana, who wanted to make the engine more powerful and sophisticated. This would have taken the car closer to its big brother the RX-7, but it would also have added weight and cost to the affordable, lightweight sports car.

The teams in Hiroshima and Irvine also clashed violently as the project approached its conclusion. Starting from March 1986, the design team at MANA had begun work on their third clay model, based on a design by Tom Matano and chief designer Koichi Hayashi, supported by Mark Jordan and Wu-Huang Chin. However, the Americans were unhappy that the car had grown in length to meet some engineering requirements, and not everyone liked the pop-ups.

Brows were furrowed as the model was sent off to Hiroshima in the summer, into the hands of senior designer Shunji Tanaka. More fireworks followed as Tanaka joined those who felt the car had outgrown its looks, and he eventually persuaded Toshihiko Hirai to reduce the wheelbase by 13mm (half an inch).

He also felt the car needed to lose some girth, although whether this weight was fat or muscle is a matter of opinion.

Tom Matano says: 'After our proposal was approved to go to production, Mr Shunji Tanaka was appointed to be the chief designer in charge of the MX-5 programme to take our theme to a realisation. During that period, he was inspired by the Noh expression as it was of true Japanese origin. He was a sculptor before taking up design, and he wanted the MX-5 to have a true Japanese origin.'

Tanaka was an enthusiast of Noh theatre, an ancient art form that makes Kabuki look like cutting-edge

Tanaka added arrows to Wu-Huang Chin's sketches indicating improvements to be made. The slightly drooping mouth was given a smile. (Mazda)

improvisation. On a stage empty but for a single pine tree, the actors wear laquered masks, and their fixed expressions are transformed by slight tilts of the head to catch the light and shadow. Tanaka was a talented sculptor, and used to create Noh masks in his spare time.

Steve Kubo says: 'Tanaka wanted to brush up the design and give it more grammar. The curvature lacked sophistication, so he smoothed it down. The MX-5 has very delicate and sophisticated lines. I've heard it has 250 faces according to the light.'

Even though he was hurt at the time that his design was altered, Tom Matano is gracious about the result. He says: 'Mr Tajima, a well-known photographer, shot photos for the Miata book of development history prior to that historical introduction in Chicago in 1989. I heard that he mentioned to the staff that the MX-5 prototype was the first Japanese car he could photograph from any angle.

'I also heard at the launch, that it was definitely not Japanese, it couldn't be an American originated design. Therefore, it must have been designed in Europe and I was pleased. We wanted Mazda Design to have an identity of its own, and the MX-5 was the first. Cars that followed had similar characteristics. I felt that we were successful in achieving our goals.'

What they said

The reaction of the press and public alike was unadulterated joy, and the enthusiasm poured from keyboards all over the world.

'The MX-5 is a perfect testament to 'oneness', the Car and Man, and Man and Technology. It is simple and straightforward, but not a nostalgic regression to a crude past. It is a thoroughly modern automobile that imparts rare individuality by the people who have the spirit of adventure.'

Jack K. Yamaguchi, *MX-5, The Rebirth of the Sportscar*, 1989 (Japan)

'You still can't help thinking that Mazda has built a car for those of us who were born too late for the English roadster craze. Thank God. That means we can have our roadster with reliability.'

US journalist Jean Lindamood writing in *Autocar & Motor*, 15 February 1989 (UK)

MX-5 v ELAN

Even now, those who don't know better will say 'The MX-5? They just copied the Lotus Elan, didn't they?'

It's true that Mazda bottled the essence spirit of Colin Chapman's original and that the new car shared a few of the engineering principles, but as the journalists writing back-to-back comparisons in the early days found, the two cars are quite different. They don't share a nut or a bolt and when parked side-by-side they don't even look similar. (Apart from having pop-up headlamps.)

The MX-5's real rival was not the old Elan, but the new one, launched in 1989. The creators of this long-awaited car took an almost opposite approach to those at Mazda, and indicate what could have happened, had a different team taken charge of its development.

On paper, it looked as though the Lotus would win any contest. It had the badge, the history and a high-tech modern design. The body had been designed by Peter Stevens, designer of the McLaren supercar and the 2002 MG TF, and it could would leave the underpowered Mazda behind on the first open stretch of road.

Westerners often observe with smug satisfaction, that the Japanese merely copy, whereas the British like to go out and invent something new (which may not work, of course). In the case of the MX-5, however, the use of proven technology shows common sense. The LWS had always been envisaged as a cheap car. Rear-wheel drive with wishbones all round might be old fashioned, but it delivered the fun.

Lotus, on the other hand, had too much to prove. Chapman had died in 1982 and the company was still struggling. A large part of the company's business was in research and development for external clients, so the new Elan had to be a showcase of modern technology.

The body was made of an advanced rigid composite. The standard engine was a 1,588cc, 16-valve 'Isuzu Lotus' unit delivering 130bhp at 7,200rpm and 105lb ft of torque; but the 165bhp Turbo SE delivered a storming drive and proved more popular.

There were squeals of disgust from the press when it was announced that the new Elan would be front-wheel drive. However, Lotus insisted this would be front-drive like no other. A new patented 'interactive wishbone' suspension was designed with the help of ex-F1 driver John Miles, in which each front suspension assembly was mounted on a separate raft made of heat-treated aluminium alloy.

On the face of it, they seemed to have succeeded. Most commentators were extremely impressed with the Elan's handling, although if anything, it was so well behaved, it was quite boring to drive.

When *Autocar* pitched it against the BBR Turbo MX-5 in 1991, the writer concluded: 'My vote goes to the Lotus … because it sets

a higher overall standard in small sports cars that few of us believed possible. If, in so doing, the Lotus Elan loses some of the fun element, then that can only be put down to the price of progress.'

A less kind quote from *Autoweek* ran: 'The engineers at Lotus have done a wonderful job of teaching this pig to dance, but at the end of the day, you're still dancing with a pig.'

In the end, the main reason for the Elan's failure was its price. In 1990, the 130bhp Elan cost £17,850, the SE £21,620. The standard Mazda 1.6i simply offered far more fun per pound at £14,925 (or £20,220 for the BBR).

The Elan ceased production in 1992. After Bugatti took the

company over from GM, a further run of 800 Series 2 cars was built from existing supplies of components in 1994.

Performance

Elan
1.6 litre 16v dohc four-cylinder Isuzu Lotus
130bhp @ 7,200rpm
105lb @ 4,200rpm
Max speed 122mph (196kph)
0–60mph 7.6sec
Urban/56mph/75mph 25.9/40.8/35.2mpg
(Urban/90kph/121kph 10.9/6.9/8.0 litres/100km)

Elan SE
1.6 litre 16v dohc four-cylinder Isuzu Lotus, water-cooled
    turbocharger with air-to-air intercooler
165bhp @ 6,600rpm
148lb ft @ 4,200rpm
Max speed 137mph (220kph)
0–60mph 6.7sec
Urban/56mph/75mph 26.2/42.2/31.8mpg
(Urban/90kph/121kph 10.8/6.7/8.9 litres/100km)

The born-again Lotus Elan appeared to hold all the aces against the MX-5 when it was first launched. (LAT)

MCL went for the obvious joke by getting topless model Linda Lusardi to pose with the MX-5 at the Earl's Court Motor Fair 1989. (LAT)

The UK launch for the MX-5 was held beneath sapphire-blue skies on the Greek mainland in 1990; it was an instant hit. (LAT)

'Its combination of communication, responsiveness, predictability and forgiveness make it the best-handling two-seater I've driven in recent memory – and my memory for such things is good.'

Dennis Simanaitis, *Road & Track*, March 1989 (USA)

'Brilliant!'

Autocar's single cover line, 14 March 1990 (UK)

'This is a sensational product: a car that people like to touch … it leaves you weak at the knees and brings a smile not only to driver and passenger but to onlookers. It is the most significant roadster of the decade: a classic in its own time.'

Donn Anderson, *Car New Zealand*, March 1990

'It's quick steering, willing engine, short-throw gearbox, taut suspension and fits-like-a-glove driving position give it an instantaneous response that conjure up memories of the old Elan, only this time the headlights work and the water pump lasts a bit longer.'

Peter Egan, *Road & Track*, November 1990 (USA)

'Its small, lithe, sexy, and best of all, it handles perfectly – factors that characterised Colin Chapman's two-seater and helped put it a generation ahead of contemporary British sports cars. It is perhaps ironic that it should be the Japanese who have recaptured the theme by providing an honest, relatively simple, rear-wheel-drive sports car at an affordable price (if you buy it in Europe or the US, that is) but then, times change.'

Car South Africa, December 1990

'Mazda's nouveau roadster has got it down pat. The MX-5 is an embodiment of the less-is-more philosophy. Its performance is moderate but honest, its styling simple yet significant, its dynamics understated but excellent.'

British journalist Mike McCarthy writing for *Wheels*, July 1992 (Australia)

'The Miata is everything a sports car needs to be. It is fun to drive and is very good-looking … It's also affordable, especially when owning a sporty four-wheeler could easily cost a nose or an eye nowadays.'

Paul Wee, *Torque Class*, February 1992 (Singapore)

The reaction both stunned and thrilled its creators:

'The best reward I get is when I see someone driving one with a big grin on their face.'

Bob Hall

DID YOU KNOW?

Alternative-fuel MX-5

Mazda built three electric MX-5s and one hydrogen-powered car to investigate the potential of these alternative fuels (and, of course as a publicity stunt). As it was laden with 16 batteries, the electric car could only manage a top speed of 80mph (129kph), crawling to 60mph (96kph) in 21.5 seconds. The hydrogen car used a rotary engine from an RX-7 and gave much better performance figures – 13.0sec 0–60mph and a top speed of 93mph (150kph), compared with figures of 8.6 sec and 119mph (191kph) for the original 1.6 MX-5.

Mazda produced three nickel-cadmium battery-powered prototypes in the early 1990s, developed jointly with the Chugohu Electric Power Company. (Andrew Fearon)

'Nobody had any idea there would be so much interest, we thought it would be a niche vehicle, but it just exploded.'

Mark Jordan

'We all felt this would never happen again. My favourite thing is to sit at events and see smiling customers having a blast.'

Norman Garrett

'It is my pleasure and beyond my expectation on the success of the MX-5 from the time of its introduction to its sustained popularity today.'

Tom Matano

'We were surprised that the MX-5 sold so well. It is the car that people were waiting for for a long time.'

Steve Kubo

Chapter **Three**

More power

'Nice car, needs more power,' was a phrase that echoed from both sides of the Atlantic as soon as the motoring hacks got their hands on the MX-5. In America, a number of owners drove straight to Rod Millen Motorsport or other kindly power brokers willing to slip a turbo under the bonnet. Millen turbo kits were then shipped abroad and were popular as far away as Australia.

The Mazda's brilliant handling made it an instant hit, but some drivers yearned for more power. (LAT)

Mazda spokesmen must have had to bite their corporate tongues as the same questions came up at every press conference or interview. Would there be a 2.0-litre? Perhaps something bigger, such as a 2.5-litre V6? Would there be a turbocharged version, after all there was a turbocharged Mazda 323?

The answer was a firm no. Handling, not performance was to be the Mazda's core value, and the power had to be kept down to keep insurance premiums low. The Mazda Corporation made its intentions clear when the MX-5 was launched at the

1989 Chicago Auto Show alongside the Club Racer concept car – which had a standard 1.6 engine. The only upgrades for its imaginary weekend racing life were a big-bore exhaust and a set of Bilstein dampers. (See page 41.)

Interviewed on the stand by *Autocar*, Tom Matano commented: 'We wanted to bring back the feeling of weekend amateur racing as well as whetting the appetites of potential buyers by letting them see how the MX-5 can be personalised.'

The journalist also tracked down a spokesman who said firmly that there would not be a turbocharged version, explaining patiently, that a turbo was 'not suitable for this type of vehicle'.

Mr Hirai actually despised turbos, because they added weight and complication, and because they had a bad reputation for reliability in Japan at the time. Plus – a turbo would ruin the carefully tuned sound of the MX-5's exhaust.

Nevertheless, having seen the tuners getting to work in the USA, and with the possibility of Rod Millen Motorsport selling kits in the UK, the British importer MCL (Mazda Cars Ltd) in Tunbridge Wells, Kent, decided to get in first, even before the MX-5's UK launch in 1990. At the time, there were rumours of a 2.0-litre model to be launched in 1992, but in the meantime, the company decided to offer an 'official' turbo, then somehow managed to persuade the parent company to back its project.

Greed for speed and the BBR Turbo

Three British heavy hitters were approached: TWR (Tom Walkinshaw Racing), Turbo Technics and Brodie Brittain Racing with a brief to create an effective, affordable kit, simple enough to be fitted by technicians at Mazda dealerships after suitable training. It was a tall order, in particular because the essential bolt-on nature of the kit meant retaining the standard car's 9.4:1 compression ratio – sky-high for a turbocharged engine.

BBR's package, using a Garrett T25 turbocharger with integral wastegate and water cooling, was deemed the best solution. It boosted power to 150bhp at 6,500rpm and torque by more than 50 per cent to 154lb ft at 5,500rpm

The kit had 68 parts and was offered by 60 selected dealers. BBR made up a new exhaust manifold of

British importer, MCL, got together with Brodie Brittain Racing to produce the 130bhp BBR Turbo. (LAT)

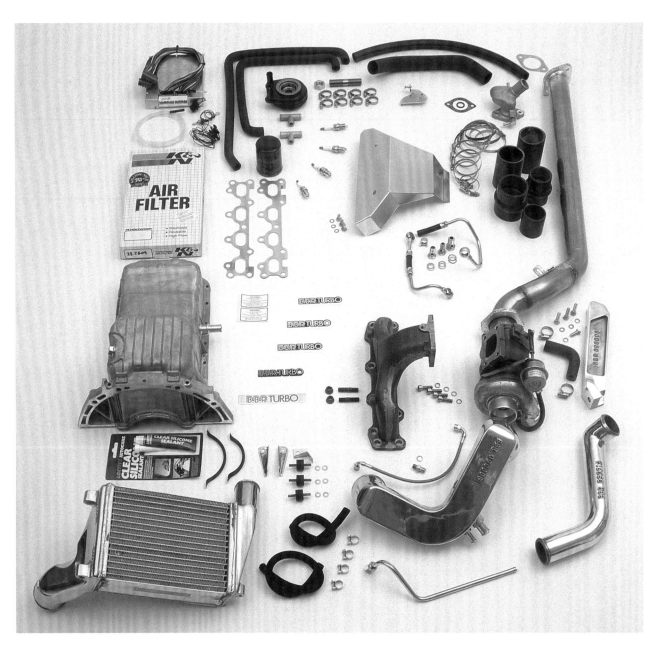

The BBR kit had 68 parts, including a Garrett T25 turbo. It could be fitted by 60 selected Mazda dealers and was covered by a full warranty. (LAT)

high-temperature alloy and added a stainless steel exhaust downpipe and heat shield. A modified sump provided a return oil feed for the turbo lubrication. To cope with the extra heat under the bonnet, pipework for the power steering, oil system and cooling were all to competition spec.

BBR's revised engine management system consisted of an auxiliary electronic brain with three-dimensional mapping to control fuel injection, ignition and boost pressure. This conversion cost £3,700 in 1990 and took 12 hours to achieve. To mark the car out visually, the proud owner drove off on special alloy wheels by Oz Racing with five flat spokes in a star pattern. The body wore a rear spoiler and BBR decals on the rear and on each wing beneath the side flashers.

Mr Hirai's reaction is not recorded, but was probably somewhere between bruised feelings and disgust when MCL persuaded the Mazda Corporation, not only to accept this conversion, but to offer Mazda's generous standard three-year or 60,000-mile warranty. It was the only conversion to receive this until the Australian MX-5 SP of 2001. The BBR conversion was also used again for the Le Mans limited edition of 1991.

The BBR Turbo went down well with British journalists. *Fast Lane* wrote: 'The new turbo package is, not to beat about the bush, staggeringly good, achieved without compromising any of the details that make the original MX-5 so appealing'. (December 1990)

Performance Car gushed: 'It's fun time! Snap the gear lever through its gate at 6,000rpm and in no time your hair will be standing on end. The engine delivers the goods in a superbly consistent rush and with no lag. You could be fooled into thinking there was a normally aspirated 2-litre engine under the bonnet.' (January 1991)

ROD MILLEN MOTORSPORT TURBO

It was so obvious, whatever Mazda's beleaguered spokesmen said. The MX-5 shared the same basic engine as the 323 Turbo. It had the same 1,597cc capacity block, the same twin-cam 16-valve head and the same fuel-injection system. And it took Rod Millen less than six months to add the turbocharger.

California-based Kiwi, Millen, had been modifying Mazdas for close to 15 years. He'd competed in most classes of motorsport, from the Daytona 24 Hours to the terrifying Pike's Peak hillcimb and wowed the rallying world with his storming 4wd RX-7. Mazda itself had acknowledged the high quality of Millen's aftermarket work and even involved him in test programmes of new models.

Millen Motorsport set to work on one of the very first Miatas to arrive in the States, but the original aim was simply to create a running showcase for potential aftermarket items.

The engine was removed and stripped, the pistons and camshafts from the 323 GTX engine were fitted and the turbocharger bolted on, with the 626 turbo intercooler fitted right down in the nose of the car for maximum airflow and efficiency.

Larger injectors from the RX-7 were added. The ECU was reprogrammed and an additional computer added. Millen's workshop fabricated a unique 2.5in stainless steel exhaust system and manifold to let it breathe. The standard radiator had to be replaced wth the slightly smaller 323 version to make room for the intercooler and its associated pipework.

The result was a power hike from 116bhp (USA) to a thumping 230bhp at 5,500rpm, all from the standard 1.6-litre engine.

As other modifiers have found since, the Mazda's chassis can cope remarkably well with more power, but it still needed to be tied down even more firmly to keep its nose and tail travelling in the right order. The Turbo was lowered an inch, with 25 per cent

The more cautious *CCC (Cars and Car Conversions)* recorded: 'Correction is often great fun in this car, as the extra power helps you hold the tail out and power out of corners at most speeds. But it does get a bit tedious if you're doing it all the time, so one tends to drive the turbo with much more concentrated circumspection on how much boot you give it. You can't really throw it at lanes with abandon.' (1991)

The car did not prove massively popular considering the thousands of standard cars snapped up in the UK. Around 750 kits were supplied in the UK and a further 150 overseas between November 1990 and September

stiffer springs and thicker roll bars mounted on urethane bushes. Sterner brake discs from the RX-7 were added to give more stopping power.

If the car hadn't been painted a lurid shade of yellow, it wouldn't have announced its presence too loudly before disappearing over the horizon. It had 15 x 7in wheels produced for Rod Millen Motorsport by Panasport in Japan, wearing Bridgestone Potenza 205/50 RE 71 VR tyres (the wheels were also painted body colour). A small lip spoiler clamped neatly to the bootlid without any drilling, and a moulded glassfibre rear deck covered up the hood when it was stowed.

Nigel Fryatt from *CCC (Cars and Car Conversions)* drove the car in the US and fell in love with it. He wrote: 'Give it too much too soon, and the obvious happens. The combination of steering and chassis response does, however, mean that the resultant indescretion can be corrected … This car deserves a fair amount of respect. Smooth is quickest for sure.'

The response to the showcase Turbo was so positive that Rod Millen Motorsport was soon offering a kit in the USA and abroad including the UK. The price was around $8,000 fitted for the USA. When it reached Australia, Greg Kable from *Modern Motor* got behind the wheel of an example wearing a more extravagant body kit including side skirts and a chin spoiler for the April 1991 issue. The tone of the feature was more measured than *CCC*, admiring the quality of the conversion, but complaining about the high price Down Under and bemoaning the loss of the standard car's friendly nature. He wrote: 'It doesn't have the nimbleness and agility that has endeared so many to the standard car.'

Nevertheless, the kits proved popular, particularly in the States, and until recently Rod Millen Motorsport sold a large range of Miata tuning parts and accessories. The company's aftermarket parts were even evaluated for the 1991 UK One-Make Challenge (see Chapter Ten). In answer to enquiries as to why this range had been dropped, a spokesman stated this was due to insufficient sales.

1991, but the number of actual conversions is unknown. It is estimated that only around 250 were made in the UK, and these cars are usually sprayed red, black or white. Some went to the USA, but did not sell well, probably because of cost.

Other options were available from BBR to improve grip, including a suspension conversion consisting of anti-roll bars front and rear with progressive-rate roll springs, a limited-slip differential plus wider, larger diameter alloys with Dunlop D40 M2 205/50ZR15 tyres.

For real speed freaks, BBR also offered a Phase II conversion, boosting power up to 240bhp, but this one was never sanctioned by Mazda or MCL.

The Phase II conversion involved a full engine rebuild with low-compression pistons, a gas-flowed and modified cylinder head, hi-flow injectors, a modified air-flow meter; fitting a larger-capacity intercooler, a full BBR 2.25in stainless steel exhaust system and extensive modifications to the engine management system. To keep these monsters on the road, BBR added a limited-slip differential, a full BBR suspension pack and a twin stainless steel 'targa bar'. Strangely, no mention is made of the brakes which had to cope with all this extra performance.

The chassis was stiffened in 1992 to improve handling and reduce vibration. (LAT)

CLUB RACER

The Club Racer Concept appeared on Mazda's 1989 Chicago Auto Show stand alongside the standard car. Painted glowing Sunburst Yellow, it gave a hint of all the weekend racing fun Miata/MX-5 owners would have. It was intended to bring back memories of low-powered, but fun and agile weekend racers such as the MG Midget and Austin-Healey Sprite, which were often raced with very little modification.

Inside, it had a racing harness for the driver and a number of switches instead of a radio. Externally it lost the pop-up headlamps, using recessed lamps set back into the wings like those of the BMW Z1.

It used the stock 1.6-litre 16v engine, so show-goers were left to imagine how they might tune and tweak it for the track.

Tom Matano said: 'We wanted to bring back the feeling of weekend amateur racing as well as whetting the appetites of potential buyers by letting them see how the MX-5 can be personalised.' At the time, the company said it had no plans to race the car, but the UK importer MCL did set up a one-make challenge in 1991. (See Chapter Ten)

Tom Matano's Club Racer concept car looked like a weekend racer, but it had a standard 1.6 engine. (Mazda)

The Club Racer's cabin had racing-style seats with four-point harnesses, inside, the stereo had been replaced by a row of switches. (Mazda)

The striking Racer appeared alongside the brand-new Miata at the Chicago Auto Show 1989. (Mazda)

The chassis was substantially stiffened again in 1994, and the 1.8 was fitted to compensate for extra weight, not to significantly improve performance; this car is a US Miata. (LAT)

Turbo performance

	Standard 1.6	BBR
Power	114bhp @ 6,500rpm	150bhp @ 6,500rpm
Torque	100lb ft @ 5,500	154lb ft 5,550rpm
0–60mph	8.76sec	6.8sec
Top speed	121mph (195kph)	130mph (209kph)

(*Autocar* could only achieve 122mph (196kph) and 0–60mph (96kph) in 10.3 seconds. BBR claimed the test car had had an incorrectly set ignition timing.)

Brodie Brittain Racing, Oxford Road, Brackley, Northants NN13 5DY UK, Tel +44 (0) 1280 702 389 Fax: +44 (0) 1280 705 339

Enter the 1.8

It might appear that Mazda had finally given in and increased the MX-5's power in 1994 when the 1.8-litre replaced the first 1.6. However, the truth is that the bigger engine only compensated for the extra weight the car had gained but things could have been different.

The MX-5 was a smash hit from launch, and local importers had kept up interest by producing their own limited editions, a process which has continued throughout the car's life. (See Chapter Seven.)

In Japan, however, the plans were more ambitious. In November 1990, Mazda set up its M2 division under Masakatsu Kato with Hirotaka Tachibana as his deputy. The division was to work on more offline projects and in December 1992 it produced the muscular MX-5 M2 1001 Roadster. The M wore a large front airdam incorporating two large round driving lamps, a rear spoiler, chromed door mirrors and a racing-style fuel filler. All were finished in a special dark blue paint and had leather seats and a leather-trimmed steering wheel. The standard 1.6-litre engine remained in place, but performance pistons raised the compression ratio to 10.57:1 and high-lift camshafts, polished ports and a less restrictive exhaust increased power to 130bhp at 6,000rpm (matching the MX-5 Challenge racers) and torque to 110lb ft at 5,500rpm. The bodyshell was stiffened and a more sporty drive was promised by its stiffer springs and tuned dampers. Its eight-spoke alloys, shod with special 195/50VR15 tyres are highly prized by hop-up merchants. The M2 was wildly popular. Only 300 were made, and after the first 200 had been sold, Mazda organised a lottery to find homes for the last 100.

This car was followed by the M2-1002 in February 1993, which had the looks, but a standard engine and no power steering. This one hardly deserved to be a success, but it also arrived just as the Japanese economy took a downturn into crisis, so the planned series of M2 cars was canned, only protoypes surviving. The programme has therefore been labelled a failure, but the M2-1002 previewed a number of important changes which soon reached the production car, including the stiffened body and Torsen differential.

The first change to the standard car came in 1992, when Mazda added a rear subframe member which reduced the infamous 65mph vibration. The modification made the rear subframe more resistant to deflection under cornering loads, so the wheels and tyres stay in better alignment with the ground.

Then in 1993, a catalytic converter was added to the UK car for the first time, blunting the 1.6 model's performance further.

The MX-5's first major change occurred first in Japan, reaching the USA and UK a year later, in a pattern that would be repeated for most major revisions. Starting from 1993 in the home market, and rippling through to the US, UK, Australia and other markets in 1994, the 1.8i and 1.8iS swept away the 1.6.

The new 1.8i's front and rear subframes were stiffened and braced. The increased structural rigidity reduced flexing in the platform and tidied up the handling, reducing nervousness on the limit, but it was at least partly deemed necessary to meet incoming side-impact regulations in the States. At the front, a transverse steel rod was installed between the lower double wishbone sub-assemblies, while two steel bars were added connecting the rear suspension to the body crossmember. In the cabin, another brace was added between the two seatbelt anchor towers.

The suspension was also fine tuned, with new dampers and bump stops, and a smaller-diameter anti-roll bar. Stopping power was improved with larger discs on each corner, 251mm in diameter at the back and 254mm at the front.

Needless to say, all this extra metal added weight, the 1.8 registering 1,040kg (2,293lb) more on the scales, than the 1.6. So the bigger engine was needed just to match the original's performance. The replacement was the 323F GT's 1.8-litre twin-cam, using hollow camshafts to reduce weight. Power was increased by 14bhp to 130bhp at 6,500rpm (128bhp in the USA), and torque was boosted by 10 per cent to 110lb ft, accessed 500rpm lower down the range at 5,000rpm. However, the new engine's rather coarse note encourages most drivers to change up well before that. The vital power-to-weight ratio was up, but only by 4bhp from 121bhp to 125bhp. At least the exhaust note remained as sweet as ever.

The snap-precision of the gearbox was also

The interior of a 1.8 Miata shows simple control layout and every owner's favourite feature, the stubby gear lever, with its 'snick-snick' action. (LAT)

THE 'LOST' M2s

The poor state of the Japanese car market and the failure of the M2 1002 put paid to Mazda's plans to produce a series of top-spec M2 cars. These could have lifted the range in the manner of BMW M Sport cars or ST series Fords.

The M2 1003 would have had a special aero deck cover, echoed later by the M Speedster. It wore BBS alloy wheels, and the interior would have been specially trimmed to match the outer high quality.

The M2 1006 was nicknamed the 'Cobraster' by Mazda insiders. Two prototypes were built, powered by the 220bhp quad-cam 3.0-litre V6 engine from the 929. This mean-looking beast had a widened body and used RX-7 rear suspension.

The M2 1028 was a one-off coupé with a squared-off tail, Ferrari style. The coupé theme was explored further with the M Coupé of 1996, but that car's styling was not as radical.

Just one more car was created with the M2 designation, the M2 1028 of 1994. This was described as a 'street competition' car and so featured a roll cage attached to the body at 10 points which considerably stiffened the structure. Its tuned 1.8-litre engine had a 10.6:1 compression ratio and produced 140bhp at 6,500rpm. It came with a detachable hard-top, but no soft-top.

Just 300 cars were offered for the Japanese market at a price of 2.8 million yen, and were snapped up within a couple of months. Of these, 115 were dark blue and 185 Chaste White – the national racing colour of Japan.

The M2 cars were intended to offer a top-spec model in the manner of the BMW M-range, but the M2 1002 was more like one of Ford's Ghia models, offering a plush interior but a standard powerplant. (Andrew Fearon)

The M2 1028 had a tuned engine producing 140bhp, just 300 were made and these were snapped up in a couple of months.

Described as a street competition car, the M2 1028 came with a roll-over bar as standard; it had a standard hard-top, but no soft-top. (brochure lent by Andrew Fearon)

The M2 1002's interior was lavishly trimmed in plush white leather, but it had no power steering. (Simon Farnhell)

The 1.8i was a back-to-basics model featuring steel wheels, wind-up windows and no power steering. (LAT)

mercifully left well alone, as were the ratios, but the final-drive was changed from 4.3:1 to 4.1:1, so the 1.8's overall gearing was higher. The extra power was fed to the rear wheels via a new Gleason Torsen limited-slip differential, which replaced the previous viscous diff.

The ride had actually improved, so although still stiff, it was compliant enough for a long wind-in-the-hair trip without shrieking muscles the next day. The rack-and-pinion steering remained as sharp and communicative as ever, so the journey was still more important than the destination for an enthusiastic MX-5 driver.

The new car's reception was warm, if not as ecstatic as the reviews of the first car, and there were grumbles that more power had not meant more performance. Sideways-merchants were also disappointed that some of the car's previous oversteer had been tamed.

Norman Garrett comments: 'The car was heavier, so it needed more oomph. Power was up, so was weight, so net acceleration was the same, but the insurance issue stayed in the mindset. Again, the aftermarket solved the problem for the serious enthusiasts – thus

Sebring Superchargers [the company Garrett set up after leaving Mazda] was born.'

Wheels writer Michael Stahl said: 'The 1.8 doesn't move the MX-5 forward so much as sideways'. (February 1994)

Autocar reported: 'The MX-5 turns into bends with the same legendary élan and soaks up mid-bend bumps as well as the old car. But where the first MX-5 would start to twitch its tail, especially in the wet, this one signals the limit more clearly and is more forgiving once you arrive there.'

At just £14,495 (close to £2,000 cheaper than the 1.6) the entry-level 1.8i wore plain 5.5J x 14in steel wheels and had pretty basic equipment, including manual windows. Its steering had no assistance, justified on the grounds that it gave a more pure, roadster experience and its steering wheel was a plain plastic hoop. The £17,395 1.8iS model offered power steering and a leather-clad wheel, airbags for driver and passenger, electric mirrors, a rheostat for the panel lights, a Clarion CRX87R detachable radio cassette unit with an electric aerial and anti-lock brakes. It was distinguished by super-light seven-spoke lighter alloy wheels, weighing in at just 10.3lb. These are highly prized by owners of other models seeking an attractive alloy wheel which actually improves handling, by reducing unsprung weight.

In both cars, the high-backed seats were replaced by new designs with an adjustable headrest, door pockets replaced the armrests and an immobiliser helped keep those vital insurance costs down.

Peter McSean wrote in *Autocar* of the base 1.8i: 'You don't need to be a purist to appreciate that this is the MX-5 getting back to where it belongs, which is as close to affordable as new two-seater, open-top sports cars get. After so many limited edition MX-5s puffed up with superfluous thises or thats, it's refreshing to see the car come back down to earth.'

It is worth noting here that most limited editions were based on the base car rather than the 1.8iS, and so lacked its safety equipment, even if other desirable cosmetic items were added. (See Chapter Seven.)

The 1.6 returns in 1995

Halfway through the decade, rivals were beginning to spring up to cash in on the roadster market which Mazda had now proved, without any doubt, existed. By 1995, the MX-5 had seen off the new Lotus Elan, but another serious rival, wearing a prestige roadster badge was about to emerage, the MGF. The smart, mid-engined 1.8 wowed the press and public alike and would remain the MX-5's closest rival.

The new Fiat Barchetta looked the part, too, but was never popular in the vital UK market because it remained a left-hand driver. BMW had followed its quirky Z1 with the muscular Z3, which was an instant success, however, none of its many guises have been as involving as an MX-5, and with its higher price and slightly executive character, it has never appealed to the same buyers.

MCL in the UK retaliated against the MGF with more limited editions, including the popular California and classy Gleneagles in 1995, and the Merlot and Monaco in 1996, which boasted in their press releases of under-cutting the MGF on price.

The razor-sharp marketing brains at Mazda Corporation decided to widen the range and slip a more affordable model beneath the 1.8-litre model and its new rivals. So the 1.6 was welcomed back, but it was a very different animal to the car its bigger-engined brother had replaced.

To maintain a gap between the two models, the new 1.6 was detuned to deliver just 88bhp, and its spec was spartan: steel wheels, no power steering, manual

MAZDA CELEBRATES THE PRANCING HORSE

Ferrari fan, Tom Matano, was in his element in 1994, when the Prancing Horse was the featured marque at the Monterey Historic Races, held at Laguna Seca.

As a neat publicity stunt, the California design team designed and built a 'Mi-Ari' special for the event.

It featured Plexiglass vents on the bonnet and ducts on the wings just like the 250 GTO of the 1960s, and the windscreen was a chopped-down racing version reminiscent of a late 1950s 250 GT Testa Rossa. An aerodynamic racing headrest formed a fin down the rear deck, a wide metal mesh stood in for the classic Ferrari egg-crate grille and it rode on classic-style wire wheels.

As often happens with concept cars, the Mi-Ari was then recycled as the M Speedster, and so only the solid tail section survives.

windows and no standard radio cassette. The body bracing and tweaked suspension of the 1.8 were omitted, which was just as well. With the weight these added, the 1.6 wouldn't have pulled the skin off a bowl of custard, let alone a rice pudding. The brake discs reverted to the original 235mm at the front and 231mm at the rear. The prices now stood at £17,395 for the 1.8iS, £14,495 for the 1.8i and just £12,995 for the 1.6i, so its appeal was obvious.

Final touches

Although there were no more major changes to the Mk1 after this, the MX-5 range underwent constant tweaks and tucks, and the limited editions kept rolling out in every market.

From 1995 in Japan and 1996 in the USA, a 133bhp Series II 1.8-litre engine was introduced, featuring a 16-bit ECU and a lightened flywheel to allow the engine to rev more freely.

From 1996, UK cars lost their chrome rings, Laguna Blue was discontinued and armrests were reinstated, replacing the unpopular door pockets. The next year, a high-level brake light appeared on the bootlid.

In the USA, the Miata now had to meet tough Federal side-impact requirements and even tougher OBD 11 emissions rules.

However, the Mk2 was now well underway, the M Speedster and M Coupé cars shown in 1995 and 1996 just giving tantalising hints that the now dated-looking roadster was about to gain a new lease of life.

Chapter **Four**

Thoroughly modern Mazda

When writing about the Mk2, it is often mentioned that sales of the old model were falling off in Japan and starting to drift in the USA. In fact, the question should not be why was the Mk1 replaced, but why wasn't it remodelled far earlier? At the time, most Japanese cars including the Toyota MR2 and Honda Civic changed their image more often and more radically than Madonna. That the Mk1 lasted eight years is proof of its success and the reluctance of Mazda to mess with a formula that was bringing in hard cash during some very difficult times.

In the early 1990s, the company invested heavily in focus groups to look at the future of the MX-5, and consulted owners' clubs worldwide, whose members were understandably anxious about the future of 'their' car. The message that came back was clear: 'Don't change what you don't have to'.

As the company was quite strapped for cash, this was probably music to the accountants' ears. Unnecessary and expensive changes would be frowned upon, but for once the enthusiasts and the suits were in agreement.

When the sensitive project was kicked off in spring 1994, Martin Leach, managing director responsible for

DID YOU KNOW?

A change of steering

The MX-5's rack-and-pinion steering was always quick and communicative, but there had been calls for improved high-speed stability and less on-centre twitchiness, so the steering ratio was switched on the S1 prototype from 15.0:1 to 17.0:1. Those who tried it, including the journalist Jack Yamaguchi, disliked the slower, more benign character and the ratio was swiftly switched back again.

Product Planning, Design and Programmes asked all four of Mazda's technical centres, in the USA, Europe, Hiroshima and the Yokohama branch opened in 1987, to submit ideas, but insisted that changes should not be too radical.

Chief engineer for the Mk1 and the creator of its superb suspension, Takao Kijima, took over as programme manager from Toshihiko Hirai, who retired to become a lecturer at Japan's National Oh-ita University. Kijima's instructions to all four studios were that the new car must retain the front-engined, rear-wheel-drive configuration of the original. Also, the dimensions had to stay true to the principles of light weight and optimum distribution of that weight to aid outstanding handling.

Frankfurt

The various styling studios had actually been working on ideas for the new car since the early 1990s. The boss of the Frankfurt studio, Arnold 'Ginger' Ostlethwaite, and fellow-Brit Peter Birtwhistle, had produced some radical concepts, examining the idea of a stripped-down, back-to-basics roadster. Their concept cars, known as the Lean Machine and Two-for-One, were closer to a Caterham or a Lotus Elise than an MX-5. The more realistic Mark One of 1992 had a smooth and simple body closely resembling a Porsche Speedster minus its aerodynamic rear fin. A Mark One alternative featured twin projector lamps frenched into the front wings in the manner of an Alfa GTV.

Reminiscing in 2002, Birtwhistle observed a little sadly that: 'By then [1994] it was clear that we had to keep close to the original, but the pop-up headlamps had to go. They were too heavy.'

He and 'Ginger' would have liked to have given the MX-5 a more aggressive look. Their concept car of 1995 had smooth lines, also reminiscent of the Porsche

Speedster – an area where they clearly agreed with Wu-Huang Chin, although their car was prettier than the wide-mouthed M Speedster.

They would also have preferred a more sophisticated interior, and suggested a curvy new centre panel using better quality plastics for the mouldings.

The final sketches showed a roadster looking rather like a plump MGB with similar recessed round headlamps, and in some of them the alloy wheels gave the impression of classic wire wheels.

California

Tom Matano's team had also been putting in plenty of homework, exploring future possibilities for the Miata. The public and fun results of this were the Mi-Ari featured at the 1994 Monterey Historic Races, the muscular M Speedster concept developed from it which appeared in 1995, and the M Coupé which followed them in 1996.

However, the most important model they produced was not seen in public. That was the so-called 'Trunk Model' produced in the early 1990s.

As might be clear from its name, this car was built to

Frankfurt studio's Mark One Concept of the early 1990s took simplicity to the extreme; the studio also produced a coupé, or Berlinetta, design for the MX-5. (LAT)

Frankfurt's sketches show a plump car resembling a 1980s MGB; no clay models were presented. (LAT)

MRA built the Trunk Model to investigate ways of creating more load space, but the resulting car looks very like the Mk2 MX-5. (Mazda)

This car had a slightly extended rear end, but the trunk inside was far from a useable rectangle.

look at ways of increasing luggage space, and it had its spare wheel stowed in a well beneath the floor – a feature which would follow through into the M Coupé and then the production Mk2. However, Matano's attention didn't stay with the rear of the car. The Trunk Model's Mk1 body had also sprouted a more pronounced sill line and the pop-up headlamps were replaced by oval headlamps. So, this car bore a very strong resemblence to the eventual Mk2.

Tom Matano says: 'On the second generation, we were faced with much more difficult tasks to get it right because the first generation was so successful in all markets.'

However, it is clear that he relished the task. He continues: 'When I saw the final model of the Mk1 after it left our hands for Japan, I was disappointed that all the careful tuning of the surfaces was lost. But in restrospect, that simplicity gave it a long life and the versatility for customising opportunities. Now we had the opportunity to do the second generation the way we wanted.'

Nevertheless, Matano knew he had to work within very tight parameters. He says: 'I knew that the Japanese team wanted a bigger change, while North American customers didn't want any changes to their cars. So, I wanted to define the level of change from the first to the second for MRA (MANA) team. I also made a list of key elements that should be carried over to the second.

'On the differentiation level; a car should be identified as an MX-5 from 100 yards away. At 50 yards away, people could not be sure whether it was the first or the second generation. Then, as a car got closer, you would know that it was the second generation. If, from 100 yards, people couldn't have identified the new car as an MX-5, or if at the 50 yards mark, people identified it as the second generation, we would have gone too far.

'The reasons why I didn't want the second to be too far off from the first was to maintain the kinship as well as the club in one piece. We destroyed the RX-7 club once; we didn't want that to happen again. If you go to any MX-5 gathering in the world, now both cars are happily mingled as siblings.'

He was keen to retain the same simplicity front and rear as the first-generation car and what he describes as the 'MX-5's very special "No one can hate it" personality'.

He says: 'There were many cars in the marketplace that lots of people love. But, there are only a few that no one can hate. Mini and Beetle are two such cars. MX-5 is certainly right up there with them, and I felt that this was one of the key success factors of the first generation that stood out.'

Along with a clay model and sketches by ex-Chrysler man Ken Saward, the Irvine Studio (now known as MRA) submitted four pages of cartoons. These starred Professor Matano, who demonstrated essential elements of the new car: Inspired sensation, Affordable, Fun and Symphony with nature, and pointed out areas of the car which lacked interest and could be improved. The Prof claimed that the chubby and cute little Miata had been working out since 1989 and should now be more toned and muscular.

Yokohama

Sketches and a clay model presented by the Yokohama office gave the MX-5 a more tapered rear end and not only retained, but exaggerated the pop-up headlamps, giving them slightly domed lids. The first sketches were very radical, showing a grey and pink futuristic dash and enormous fantasy wheels wearing rubber so thin it would have had to be painted on. The more realistic model was a simpler shape than the eventual Mk2, but wore a black styling stripe down the side.

Clay modellers working in MRA's California studio in Irvine. (Mazda)

Hiroshima's model had surprised-looking upright circular headlamps; it was developed into Theme A. (Mazda)

Hiroshima

Head of this team was Koichi Hayashi, now assistant programme manager, Design for Sports Cars. Having worked on the original car and loved it dearly, he found even thinking about a replacement difficult. However, he'd never liked the pop-up headlamps, and told Bob Hall with some glee that they had been despatched. Instead, the car produced by Hiroshima (known as MC, for Mazda Corporation) had round headlamps, leaning backwards in the manner of Porsche 911 lamps. The body shape was less cuddly than a Mk1, but still very simple.

Choosing a theme

Leach and Kijima were spoiled for choice when faced with the entries. All four studios had captured the spirit required, and suggested interesting features, but this had to be narrowed down. Three were selected to be converted into full-sized models at their respective studios by January 1995. These were evaluated and two, Hiroshima's proposal, to be known as Theme A, and Irvine's design, Theme B, were selected for further development.

MRA's car had fixed headlamps and a low, wide mouth; the lines of its body were close to the Trunk Model. (Mazda)

Yokohama's full-size clay model retained pop-up headlamps and the original chrome door handles. (Mazda)

M SPEEDSTER 1995

The dramatic M Speedster, unveiled at the 1995 Chicago Auto Show, gave a glimpse of what the MX-5 could have become as a response to the much-anticipated BMW Z3, and other roadsters now roaring on to the MX-5's territory. At the Geneva Show just a month later, the MX-5 saw the debuts of the MGF, Fiat Barchetta and the bare-essentials Renault Spider.

Mazda's Speedster took its name from the 1950s Porsche so beloved by racers including James Dean – who sadly died in one. Its racing intent was evident from the twin racing headrests and solid racing bucket seats fitted with four-point harnesses. The seats, steering wheel and gearknob were leather-trimmed with red stitching. Beneath the headrests, which were cunningly hinged in the centre, were two racing helmets painted deep metallic red to match the body colour.

Its 1.8-litre engine delivered 200bhp with the help of a Lysholm compressor, usually the source of power and fuel efficiency in the Millenia S Miller-cycle engine, but in this application used as an ultra high-efficiency supercharger. Using a compression ratio of 9.0:1, its peak power was delivered at 6,500rpm, and it delivered 165lb ft of torque at 5,500rpm. The taut, muscular body was designed by Wu-Huang Chin, although his starting point was the already substantially modified Mi-ari.

A low, purposeful stance is given by a half-inch wider track, achieved by using more heavily offset wheels and modified suspension using 30 per cent stiffer springs, thicker anti-roll bars and adjustable Koni shock absorbers with a variable ride-height facility. The wheels themselves were attractive five-spoke alloys equipped with larger brakes; 250mm ventilated discs at the front and 225mm solid discs at the rear would provide ample stopping power.

The door has a graceful downward sweep, much like that of the RX-7, and flaring sills meet wider wings. At the front, four projector-beam headlamps peer from beneath lids which only need to pop-up halfway, but two over-sized driving lamps glare from either side of the grille 'mouth'. In an interview with *Autocar*, Tom Matano said that these give the impression that the car is breathing out hard during a work-out.

The twin headlamps have since become one of the MX-5 modifiers' favourite options, and several companies have offered a copy-cat aero-deck panel.

In the USA, the public was given a free-phone number to give their comments. The response may have persuaded Mazda that more power was not the way to go.

The monster engine delivers 200bhp at 6,500rpm thanks to a Lysholm compressor operating as a supercharger.

The radical M Speedster has inspired many modifiers with its aero deck and twin lamps beneath half-closed 'eyes'. (Mazda)

Designed by Wu-Huang Chin, the Speedster was first shown in 1995; its door line reflects that of the RX-7. (Mazda)

A pair of racing helmets in a matching colour are stashed beneath the headrests. (Mazda)

The Theme A final mock-up resembled an Alfa Duetto. It was very pretty, but its retro look didn't fit the brief for an updated MX-5. (Mazda)

Hayashi tries the final seating buck for size. It's still a tight fit for European six-footers. (Mazda)

The full-size mock-up of Theme B looks very close to the finished product. (Mazda)

Theme A still had 911-style headlamps and as it was refined, it gained a Porsche-like nose and chin spoiler. Its door had a curved rear edge similar to that of the the M Speedster and M Coupé, which not only looked attractive, but allowed more space for body strengthening.

Matano's Theme B strongly resembled the Trunk Model, and the production Mk2 can clearly be seen in its lines. Its headlamps were already the distinctive oval 'eyes' of the 1998 car housing auxiliary lamps within them. The sill line was also stronger and sculpted, although the line was to be refined further. The biggest difference was its lower and larger 'mouth', which is actually closer to the eventual 'five-point grille' opening of the Mk3.

California's Theme B was a clear winner, and from there it was taken to Hiroshima for further refinement under Mr Hayashi.

As before, meshing design and engineering needs were difficult, and sometimes led to fireworks. Kijima and Hayashi were both happy about widening the track by 10mm at the front and 20mm at the rear. This would be better for handling, and it would balance the look of the car now its 'shoulders' had developed. However, they then clashed violently because Hayashi wanted to make the wings 3mm wider – so adding size and weight. He won, and the car eventually grew by 5mm.

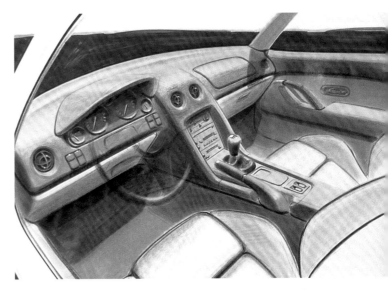

Initial sketches explored some different ideas for the dashboard and centre console shapes. (Mazda)

Interior design

It is interesting to note that when the first proposals were submitted in 1995, all four studios gave in much more colourful interiors, featuring two-tone seats and even two-tone dashboards.

Italian specialist Nardi adapted an SRS airbag installation for its three-spoke design to be fitted in the MX-5. (Mazda)

Conservatism and costs won out, however. The quality of plastics and fabrics are much improved in the Mk2 and the dash has a few more curves, but the dials have no silver surrounds.

No more space was offered for tall drivers, either. The cabin remained as simple as before – and ripe for aftermarket accessories.

Practical choices

Kijima drove and assessed plenty of competitors, and consulted Mr Hirai at the beginning of the project. His aim was to keep all the best features of the original car, and improve on its weaknesses. He wrote in an essay: 'We must value and assert the MX-5's unborn soul and train, strengthen and refine the body'.

Because money was tight, around 40 per cent of the second-generation car's body was carried over from the original. Among the sections to be retained were the windscreen, its surround and most of the front bulkhead. That meant the old hard-top could be used, saving money for both development and production costs – it was also good news for owners looking for a cheap second-hand hard-top.

Some of the changes made to the Mk2 were forced by practicality. For example, new safety regulations insisted on better crash resistance and airbags, emissions controls were also getting tighter – and all these things added weight.

In response, the engineers had to reduce weight everywhere they could, shaving fractions of kilograms from engine components, a hollow steering shaft, brace bars and even a smaller horn. Just 2–3kg saved in the construction of the seats, tyres and hood were a major victory.

Kijima said: 'It's hard work to find the balance between strength and weight, but to make an all-aluminium chassis like the (Lotus) Elise would make the car too expensive'.

More luggage space was essential, and much of the work to achieve it had already been done in California with the Trunk Model project. The spare wheel and battery, previously inside the boot, where now housed below it, not only creating space, but also lowering the centre of gravity.

The pop-ups were no longer necessary because headlamp technology had moved on, and again, the Irvine studio had studied the options and come up with a smart and modern solution. The oval lamps were one

The Mk2 improved on the handling fun of the original. (LAT)

step further down the route from the paired headlamps beneath half-opened lids featured in the M Speedster and M Coupé and had already been featured in the Trunk Model.

There were howls of anguish from traditionalists when the car was first revealed, but to keep the pop-ups now would have been purely for effect, and because they were heavy and added the complication of more moving parts, they had to go.

Another much-mourned feature to disappear was the old car's cute, oval door handles inside and out, but the decision had been made to make the new car look more modern, so the shiny retro items were replaced by body-colour handles on the outside and plastic inside. These lacked the beauty of the old ones, but it has to be said, they are easier to use and break fewer fingernails.

A glass window with a heated element for chilly days was also clearly desirable but an electric hood would add cost, and went against the principle of simplicity. Instead, Mazda's team concentrated on making the manual action easier. So, unlike the plastic window, the glass item does not need to be zipped out before the roof is lowered, and the roof is actually lighter than the old one.

Because the windscreen surround remained the same, the new hood with its glass window can be fitted to a Mk1 with some conversion work. (See Chapter Eleven.)

Improving agility

The ability to eat corners for breakfast and plant a huge grin on the driver's face was, of course, paramount. To retain this ability and even improve on it was a remarkable achievement.

Every aspect of the car had to add up to a perfect 50/50 front-to-rear weight distribution, and the body was considerably stiffened, although this was another source of unwanted weight for Kijima to have to deal with.

Kato's PPF 'spine' was retained, along with the wishbone suspension set-up, but the suspension was further tuned. To optimise driving pleasure and increase stability, front suspension geometry changes focussed on lowering the roll centre of the car and increasing the caster trail by moving the upper control arms rearward and the lower ones forward. The planted-on-the-tarmac feel was also helped by the wider track.

The Mk2 was launched at the Tokyo Motor Show in 1997 and the Eunos name was dropped. (LAT)

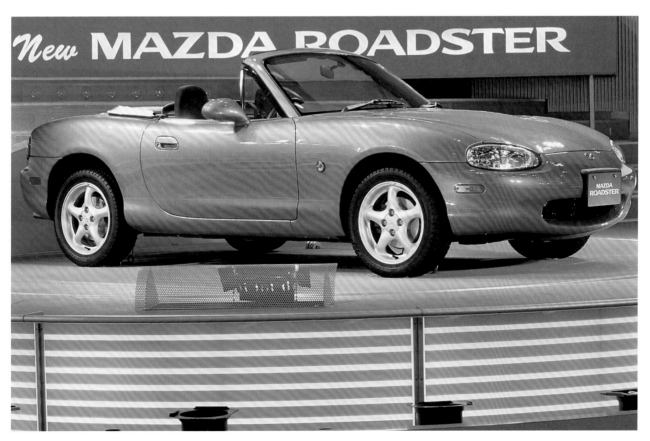

A Torsen limited-slip differential became standard on the 1.8 model and the 1.6 Special Package offered on the Japanese 1.8 Mazda Roadster (the Eunos name was dropped).

As a result of the many well-considered tweaks, the Mk2 was now able to string together a series of fast, sweeping corners far better than a Mk1. The damping was much improved and coped better with bumps and rough surfaces when the suspension was loaded up in a corner.

Some drivers felt the handling was not as sharp as it had been, and enthusiasts missed the power slides which were so easy to provoke on the early Mk1. However, at the extreme, the Mk2 was more forgiving, leaning gradually into an understeering attitude, which is less likely to catch out an inexperienced driver.

The MX-5 no longer had the stage to itself; the new model had to do battle with the Fiat Barchetta, BMW Z3 and MGF. (LAT)

The steering remained as communicative as ever, but thanks to a few minor tweaks, it felt a touch lighter and more direct. The new Nardi steering wheel for the 1.8 now housed an airbag.

Power

Once again, the option of a larger engine and its associated costs were firmly resisted. The new car was launched with the existing 1.8 and 1.6 engines, but Mazda's hot rodders had been at work once again.

A new cylinder head was cast, featuring a more upright intake port to improve breathing and combustion. A lighter flywheel was fitted along with new pistons to give a higher compression ratio and the camshaft was given new profiles. A remapped ECU ensured the engine made the most of its power. Plus the breathing was improved, with improvements including the use of Mazda's variable inertia charge induction system (VICS).

The 1,839cc BP-2E (RS) unit now had 10 per cent

M COUPÉ 1996

Tom Matano teased visitors to the 1996 New York Auto Show with a coupé concept for the MX-5 in the mould of the MGB GT, or Triumph GT6. This was, in fact, something BMW went on to do, when it added the hot-shoe M Coupé to its Z3 range.

The hard-top might not have made it into production, but this car revealed some features to be carried over into the Mk2 Roadster. The most important of these was a larger boot, with a spare wheel stowed beneath the floor, which had developed for the secret experimental Trunk Model.

The Coupé borrowed its door line, sill moulding and twin-projector beam headlamps of the 1995 Speedster. It also had the same wider track, but wore different wide-rim five-spoke alloys shod with 205/45 R16 Dunlop SP8000 tyres.

Unlike the Speedster, it used a stock 133bhp 1.8-litre engine. Its overall shape was smoother and more elegant, too, in contrast to the previous car with its crouching stance and the cigar-chomping look given by the lower driving lamps.

As this was purely a show car, the roof was made of glassfibre, but featured a very large sloping rear window to achieve excellent visibility. Inside, a folding rack was provided behind the seats to hold some small items of luggage.

Coupé shared the twin headlamps of the Speedster, but the nose shape was far closer to the production car. (Mazda)

GT6-style M Coupé of 1996 profile shares door, and extended sill line with the M Speedster, but it is a more elegant shape. (Mazda)

more power, 140bhp at 6,500rpm and 119lb ft of torque at 4,500rpm. The 1,597cc BE-2E (RS) unit delivered 108bhp at 6,500rpm and 99lb ft at 5,000rpm.

Neither engine was the smoothest nor the most responsive around, however both were now punchier and more flexible than before.

Six appeal

A number of manufacturers were working on six-speed gearboxes at this time, but the upper echelons at Mazda didn't seek one out.

Some of the younger engineers actually conspired, instead, to make it happen. The gearbox manufacturer Aisin-AI, based in Nagoya, Japan was known for its work with Toyota. The company was interested in developing a six-speed box for a front-engined, rear-wheel-drive car, but Toyota didn't have anything that fitted the bill. Needless to say, the company was

delighted to be given an MX-5 mule to work on, and so the development of the Y16M-D gearbox began.

When a prototype six-speed gearbox was delivered and fitted to a factory MX-5, the Mazda team knew they had to grab it. Sadly, only Japanese buyers were able to have this transmission on a mainstream 1.8-litre model. The rest of the world only had the chance to try it in the 10th Anniversary Mk2.

Europeans could not order an automatic, either. However, no one ever had any complaints about the five-speed box, and, thanks to reworked synchros, this felt slicker than ever.

Wheels and tyres

The standard wheel and tyre combination for the new car was a set of pressed steel four-bolt 14 x 6JJ wheels, except for the Japanese entry-level model, which had 14 x 5.5JJ wheels. Higher-spec models were given cast aluminium five-spoke, four-bolt 15 X 6JJ items. The tyres for both options were once again a lightweight design, weighing in at 0.6kg less for the 15in wheel and 0.5kg less for the 14in.

The Mk2 had revised rear lights. This photograph was taken at the Chobham test track, where IAD first demonstrated the V705 for Mazda's US team. (LAT)

The brakes were 255mm diameter ventilated discs at the front and 251mm solid discs at the rear. Anti-lock brakes were standard on the 1.8-litre model in Europe and the higher-spec models for both engine sizes in Japan; it was optional in the States.

Mk2 unveiled

The new car was unveiled at the 1997 Tokyo Motor Show, and went on sale in Japan and the USA that year, reaching the UK in 1998. It looked so similar to the original that some journalists referred to a mere 'face-lift' when, in fact, almost every element of the car had been studied and refined if not changed altogether.

Once enthusiasts got over the loss of the original and sat in the driving seat, however, the reaction was enthusiastic.

'It's an appreciation that creeps up on you slowly and then pulls into sharp focus when you come across an old model, which suddenly looks dated.'

John Barker, *Performance Car*, 1998 (UK)

'It really does feel more like a new car than anyone would imagine from looking at it … The biggest improvement, though is in the handling. When you cornered hard in its predecessor, understeer set in early and if you tried to slide the tail out, it could catch out the unwary by suddenly snapping into oversteer when the suspension bottomed out. The new MX-5 understeers less and … its easier and more controllable to drift.'

Yasushi Ishiwatari, *Top Gear*, 1998 (UK)

'There's nothing small or dainty about the driving experience any more. It's fast, focussed and fun'.

David Vivian, *Autocar*, 1998 (UK)

'It's behaviour was impressive, with a more taut feel that communicated the more seat-of-the-pants sensation of our old car … Simply put, it's about the purest driving experience you can have in a modern production car.'

Douglas Knott, *Road & Track Special*, 1998 (USA)

Brochure shows the ease of roof operation, plus the new standard windblocker. (Simon Farnhell)

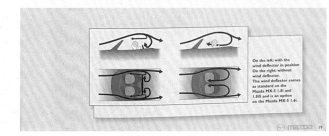

Chapter Five

The Mk2 gets
a face-lift

The 2001 MX-5 is known to some as the Mk2.5 because it looks so similar to the previous incarnation, but this is a vital model for Mazda and it has been substantially reworked under the skin to make sure it can still keep its nose ahead of marauding pretenders to its crown.

The biggest upcoming rival was the MG TF, given a

The MX-5 needed a face-lift to freshen up its image as its closest rival, the MGF was morphing into the more macho MG TF. (Simon Farnhell)

face-lift by Peter Stevens (ironically designer of the MX-5's first rival, the Lotus Elan). Mazda knew the TF's mid-mounted engine would be more powerful than before and its hydragas suspenion was to be dumped for a sharper set-up to deliver better handling (although, in the event, it turned out to be bone-jarring).

The new MX-5 was designed entirely in Japan, although the studios in Frankfurt and Irvine were consulted in advance on what their local customers would want. The views of the owners' clubs were also taken into consideration, and there was one clear

Inspire? Stimulate? Soar? You ask for it, the Mazda MX-5 Miata delivers. Built as a pure sports car from the first pixel on an engineer's computer screen, this two-seat, drop-top roadster combines a DOHC engine that loves the redline with reflex-quick handling. And it's ready for action whenever you want some.

WHICH VERB WOULD YOU LIKE TO EXPERIENCE TODAY?

message – we like it the way it is. Keep 'em coming, but don't spoil our car.

The company could have left the styling alone and slipped in a more powerful engine to take on its rivals, but Mazda stuck to the same principles laid down at the very beginning. The LWS would remain cheap to buy, run and insure, so the new car would stick with 1.6 and 1.8 engines.

However, the 1.8 would now benefit from sequential valve timing (S-VT), to deliver optimum performance and efficiency, taking its peak power up to its highest ever in the UK: 145bhp at 7,000rpm and 124lb ft of torque at 5,000rpm. The result is a claimed acceleration of 0–62mph in 8.4 seconds and a top speed of 129mph. The power is delivered to the road using the same stubby lever, but owners get a choice of five or six ratios, and UK buyers have the option of a four-speed automatic for the first time.

The biggest visual change is the 'mouth' which has given rise to the tag 'Sharknose'. The stretched opening echoes the new five-point grille seen on other new Mazda models, as Tom Matano says: 'We wanted to align the front design with other Mazda cars to strengthen the brand identity. We also intended to add a little stronger personality to meet a market request in Japan and USA.'

Peter Birtwhistle from the Frankfurt studio comments: 'It has that same tension in space as the grille on other cars, but it doesn't need the grille itself. Brand recognition is important, but the sports car models (MX-5 and RX-8) can survive well enough without having Mazda stamped all over them.'

He explains that the new car's headlamps were given new reflectors and projector lamps beneath a clear glass cover 'to give it more interest at the front'. The rear lamp clusters have also been revised.

Birtwhistle would have liked to have seen a brighter and more interesting cabin, but again the designers in Japan stuck to the traditional recipe. At least the dash is brightened by white dials and chrome surrounds – just like the accessory items fitted by many enthusiastic owners. New high-backed seats became standard, and buyers were promised a good level of equipment for the price, too, including good safety and security equipment. The 1.8 was also treated to some new 16-inch aluminium wheels.

The most important differences are not so

The change was so subtle, some people called this new car the Mk2.5; its new grille was designed to echo the then new five-point Mazda family grille. (Mazda)

MX-5 MPS

Mazda presented the promise of a high-performance and sporty future at the 2001 Frankfurt Motor Show. The rotary-engined RX-8 Concept appeared alongside the red-and-hot MX-5 MPS Concept, plus the 323 MPS.

MPS stands for Mazda Performance Series, and the designation could eventually be used on many more cars in the range. The American version of the 323 MPS, known as the MP3, has already become a favourite with the Japanese-car street-racing fanatics portrayed in the film *The Fast and the Furious.*

The MX-5 MPS was created to boost the sporting reputation of its rather milder brother, the newly launched MX-5 Mk3 and to help Mazda gauge the demand for a more powerful version of that car.

A Formula 4 1,930cc engine growled from beneath the bonnet, benefiting from Mazda Speed racing technology to lift the power to 180bhp at 7,000rpm, and torque to 150lb ft at 6,000rpm. For quicker throttle response and higher output, four independent throttles and high-lift camshafts were adopted, yielding a piston speed of 19.8m/second. The power was fed to the wheels via a six-speed gearbox.

The suspension was modied with height-adjustable mono-tube dampers and springs to give even flatter cornering and increased grip. The front and rear suspension mountings points were reinforced with lightweight aluminium for enhanced rigidity. The Torsen limited-slip differential was also replaced by a prototype which tames the usual tailswing. Impressive 17 x 7J alloy wheels wore ultra-low-profile 215/40 R17 tyres while monster 314mm brake discs, ventilated at the front, hauled the MPS up sharp.

Road & Track drove the car in Japan, reporting: 'Turn-in is exceptionally crisp, with the car exhibiting flawless balance through all types of corners.'

A body kit not only gave an aggressive, lower and wider look, but also helped gravity keep the car glued to the road. Air outlets in the wings were designed to reduce air pressure inside and under the body to reduce rear-end lift, and a lip spoiler on the boot increased downforce at speed.

Inside, the lucky driver sat on a combination black buckskin and Alcantara fabric seat and faced a sporty console featuring Alumite-finish metallic details.

Positive reaction to the MPS means a version of this car may possibly appear as a special edition in the future, although it will probably have a little less power to keep emissions and ever-threatening insurance ratings down.

However, just as Mazda in Australia has now answered the pleas of those craving for more power with the SP (see page 67), engineers at Ford in Detroit have toyed with the idea of a V6 Miata. A 210bhp version of Ford's 3.0-litre aluminium-block V6 was squeezed into an experimental monster called the Miata Detroit, also driven by *Road & Track.* Wearing a huge bonnet scoop like the muscle cars of old, the Detroit could reach 60mph in 5.8 seconds. Its peak power punched in at 6,500rpm, it produced 205lb ft of torque at 4,750rpm, and to handle it, the standard gearbox was replaced by the RX-7's five-speeder. *R&T* wrote: 'Once (the tyres) grab a bite of tarmac, hang on, because the car snaps forward like a hot rod, lifting the car's front end slightly in the process.'

Could this idea develop into a next-generation MX-5 to challenge high-performance Europeans such as Porsche and BMW? We'll have to wait and see.

A hot MPS version of the MX-5 appeared alongside the new RX-8 at the Frankfurt Motor Show in 2001; Mazda was keen to hear whether owners wanted a performance flagship for the MX-5. (Mazda)

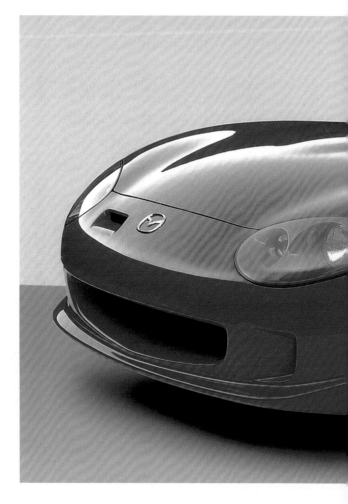

Power was slightly up, and the handling was even sharper than before; the six-speed gearbox was now offered in the UK. (LAT)

immediately obvious, however: the quality of the build and materials are better than ever, and although the engine doesn't feel obviously more powerful, it seems sharper, and revs with real verve. To give it a snappier

The space-saver spare wheel is stowed beneath the floor as in the Mk2. (LAT)

throttle response and a wider, more useable power band, the engine was given reshaped pistons and a higher compression ratio. An improved intake manifold and adjustments to reduce intake and exhaust resistance make its breathing a little easier.

The Mk3's handling also has edged closer to its roots, having grown gradually softer to accommmodate American tastes and has regained some of the energy and agility of its youth.

To strengthen and stiffen the body, the side sills, tunnel gussets and other structural elements have been enlarged and thickened. The sporty double-wishbone set-up was retained, but the suspension was fine-tuned, tweaks including modifications to the shock damping force and the option of Bilstein dampers for the 1.8 Sport. The brakes were also uprated, the master cylinder, vacuum booster and brake discs all growing in size on the 1.8. Anti-lock brakes with electronic brake-force distribution (EBD) help keep the car on the road in the most extreme situations.

As a result, it is as nimble and fluid on a series of curves as a greyhound with a rabbit in its sights, and its quick, communicative steering, precise gearchange and firm brakes make the driver feel as though the car is being operated by telepathy.

The six-speed gearbox allows quieter, more economical cruising on the motorway, but it is not

AUSSIE MX-5 SP

Just like MCL in 1991, Mazda Australia has decided to quench the thirst of muscle-mad customers in its own market, by offering a locally developed, turbocharged MX-5 with a full Mazda warranty.

The 1.8-litre MX-5 SP went on sale in January 2002. Its 150kW (201bhp) and 280Nm (207lb ft) earn it the designation SP for Sports Performance, a badge previously worn by hot models of the RX-7 and Eunos 800.

It was developed by Sydney-based Mazda motorsport manager, Allan Horsley, who masterminded the company's many famous RX-7 wins in both touring cars and at the Bathurst 12-hour production car race. The cars are assembled for Mazda by Prodrive in Melbourne.

Mazda Australia's managing director, Malcolm Gough, announced that the six-speed manual MX-5 SP would go on sale priced at $55,540. Air-conditioning remains a $200 option, as some buyers are bound to head straight for the nearest race track.

Visual enhancements included a chrome fuel filler cap and scuff plates and an alloy gearknob and gear lever surround.

Gough said: 'This car will satisfy those MX-5 fans that have craved even more performance than that delivered by the standard model. However, the SP has been carefully developed to ensure that this MX-5 is as delightful to drive everyday as the non-turbo car.'

Allan Horsley adds: 'From day one, our goal was to deliver a car with a progressive, lag-free, user-friendly power and torque curve. By employing a relatively low-boost system and with careful engine tuning, aided by a remapped ECU, we have been able to achieve our goal while delivering at least 33 per cent more power, Perhaps even more significant is the 55 per cent improvement in torque.'

The SP uses the same S-VT 1.8-litre engine as the standard Mk3, but more than 215 parts are added or modified during the conversion. Boost comes from a water-cooled Garrett turbocharger. New fuel injectors are fitted, and the ability to expel exhaust gases from the engine has been improved by a free-flowing heavier-duty manifold.

Other changes include a larger radiator, oil-return line from the turbo to the sump, new spark plugs and a big-bore exhaust system with a deeper, sportier exhaust note.

Mazda Australia originally planned to build 100 MX-5 SPs, but the response has been so enthusiastic, this will probably be increased.

The SP will be covered by the same comprehensive three-year/unlimited warranty as other Mazda passenger cars.

For a crazier, non-official muscle Mazda, Australian power nuts can also buy Lexus V8-powered MX-5s from Bullet Cars (see Chapter Eleven).

Mazda SP performance data

Engine: inline, 1,839cc 4-cyl DOHC 16V, turbocharged and intercooled
Bore and stroke: 83.0 x 85.0mm
Compression ratio: 10.0:1
Max power: 201bhp (approx) @ 6,800rpm
Max torque: 207lb ft (approx) @ 4,600rpm
Brakes: front 270mm disc ventilated; rear 276mm
Kerb weight: 1,119kg (2,467lb)

The Australian SP (Sports Performance) was the first official MX-5 turbo to be offered since the BBR Turbo of 1991. (Mazda Australia)

The SP was developed by Mazda Australia's Motorsport Division. It develops 33 per cent more power and 55 per cent more torque than the standard car. (Mazda Australia)

universally loved. It needs plenty of stirring to keep within the power band, and it has a disconcerting dogleg when changing down from sixth to fifth. Having sixth apparently opposite reverse is a little worrying, too. However, as with all quirks, owners soon get used to it.

Safety is better than ever. Mazda's advanced impact-energy distribution and absorption system protects occupants, standard twin airbags and three-point seatbelts with pretensioners on all models protect the little roadsters in case of an accident.

Opinions on whether the Mk3 can floor the MG TF and Toyota MR2 vary widely. The enthusiasts at *Autocar* forgave the MG TF its bouncy ride and put it on the top step of the podium. Steve Sutcliffe described the new MX-5 1.8i Sport as: 'The more grown up, purely because it is less frenetic. It rides exceptionally well, with no shimmy and a lot of control.'

The monthly magazine, *EVO*, put the MR2 at the top of its pyramid, followed by the MX-5. the TF's

The body of the new car was stronger and stiffer, the suspension was fine-tuned and the brakes improved. (Mazda)

predecessor, the 160bhp MGF Trophy came third labelled as a 'softy' because of its hydragas suspension.

However, the monthly *What Car?,* felt that most people couldn't live happily with the MG TF's uncomfortable ride and planted the MX-5 firmly at the top, ahead of both the MG and Peugeot 206 CC, praising its pure fun and value for money.

MX-5 Mk3 in the UK

The MX-5 was introduced at a very difficult time for Mazda in the UK. In 2000, sales were falling worldwide and franchised dealers all over Britain were deserting the sinking ship, leaving large areas without a Mazda representative.

As a result, distribution was taken away from MCL and will now be dealt with directly from Europe. In 2002, Mazda was trying to revitalise the dealer network and promoting the brand relentlessly with TV advertisements and press events.

The change actually brings the UK owner's club closer to the action, because its contact point is now Mazda Europe in Frankfurt rather than an importing

agent, and representatives were invited to a major party at Easter 2002 in order for their views to be heard.

One major change for future buyers is that Limited Editions will now be Europe-wide models created in Frankfurt rather than individual UK models. The first to appear was the Phoenix in March 2002 (see Chapter Eleven). This used the same grey metallic paint and Saddle Brown leather colour scheme as the US SE Titanium Gray and the Australian Titanium. Unusually for a UK special, it was available as a 1.6 or 1.8 and was loaded with a standard kit, whereas UK limited editions were previously often based on entry-level models.

Where to now?

The good news for enthusiasts everywhere is that we can probably look forward not just to the next generation MX-5, but many more. Tom Matano confirmed that a new car is already on the drawing board, although he could not release any details yet.

Mazda has a great deal of work to do first. The company freely admits that it made a big mistake in the mid-1990s, by paying too much close attention to focus

groups and trying to compete with volume manufacturers. The resulting products were conservative, bland and lacking in the passion of the MX-5, RX-7 or Xedos 6.

'It was very frustrating for the design community,' says Frankfurt designer Peter Birtwhistle: 'The last 626 would have made a perfect surveillance car. No one saw you arrive, no one saw you leave and no one ever knew you were there.'

Now the company is going back to its roots, and hopes to establish itself as the sporty marque – perhaps the Alfa Romeo – of the Ford group. Its future products will aim to be unconventional, daring and different. The first result of the new attitude is the Mazda6. This handsome family segment machine is intended to be a driver's car, and its suspension has been tweaked and tuned by Phillip Martens, who worked with chassis guru Richard Parry-Jones on the sharp-handling Ford Mondeo.

With luck this all means that those working on the new MX-5 will have the same freedom as the original

From the rear, you would be hard-pressed to spot that this is a Mk3. (Mazda)

The cabin quality has been improved and the Mk3 has attractive white dials with chrome surrounds, just like the aftermarket versions many owners had fitted previously. (Mazda)

team, but with more support. It doesn't mean the baby will be thrown out with the bathwater, however.

Peter Birtwhistle says: 'Business sense says Mazda should refine it [the MX-5] and do a 911, allowing it to evolve through the generations.'

The MX-5 MPS was shown at Frankfurt in 2001 to help Mazda canvas opinions about the idea of a hotter car, but the main response seems to have been once again, that people love the car as it is. If they want a

DID YOU KNOW?

Best-selling sports car

The MX-5 has entered the *Guinness Book of World Records* as the best-selling sports car ever, with over 600,000 sold. It has a long way to go to catch up with some other automotive favourites though. More than 21 million old-style VW Beetles have been made, and 5.3 million original Minis were produced before it was replaced by the BMW version.

high-powered car, they can buy the RX-7. The exception to this rule seems to be in Australia, where Mazda has agreed to offer a warranty on the turbocharged MX-5 PS, created by the local distributor and Tickford in the manner of MCL and the BBR Turbo back in 1991.

Birtwhistle observes: 'Lots of customers – including an important number of female buyers like the car the way it is, they don't want anything too aggressive, and they like its compact dimensions and comfort. The MX-5 doesn't offend anyone. If a BMW Z3 driver sees a Porsche Boxster, there's a bit of a needle there, but they'd both wave happily at the MX-5 driver.'

Mazda designers, engineers and managers are taking every opportunity to attend events, meet the owners, chat and listen to the views of their customers.

Birtwhistle says: 'We listen to what they want, we need to understand what they want – it's very valuable information.'

As this book goes to press, the MX-5 has sold more than 600,000 worldwide and is carving itself an unassailable position in the *Guinness Book of World Records*. The new one will be shaped with the help of those who know it best – its drivers.

Chapter Six

Choosing and buying an MX-5

If you have decided to buy an MX-5, you've already made the right decision. The Mazda is tough, reliable and likely to have been loved and cared for by its previous owners. Plus, it holds its value, so you won't be throwing your money away.

It may have brought the spirit of freedom and enjoyment of the classic roadsters from the 1960s, but it left behind the rust, the bad-tempered electrics and reluctance to go out in the wet. If well looked after, it must be one of the most reliable cars on the market.

The engines are happy to rack up hundreds of thousands of miles and – unusually for a sports car – there are plenty of dealers to keep up that collection of regular dealer service stamps.

Running costs are surprisingly modest. The Mazda's simplicity also means that servicing and regular parts are comparable with a basic hatchback, and thanks to forward planning by its creators, insurance premiums will cost less than most hot hatches. The owners' club will also be able to offer you a very good insurance deal.

Your national owners' club can also help you find your car, so it's a good idea to sign up even before you get your hands on a set of keys. You'll be able to find general advice on club websites and in the magazine, which will also have ads for cars for sale. And you'll find a friendly ear if you need help.

Make sure you look through plenty of classified ads to get a good idea of what to pay (again the owner's club websites should be able to give you up-to-date estimates). Prices tend to dip in winter as buyers aren't in the roadster frame of mind, and as Christmas approaches buying a car gets pushed to the back by the need to find a Buzz Lightyear or the precise Pokemon. As the bulbs start to come up in spring, so do MX-5 prices.

However, one of the greatest advantages the MX-5 hunter has is that there are so many very good cars

Read up before you buy; early cars like this Mk1 are now officially classed as classics. (Simon Farnhell)

Mazda MX-5

around to choose from. By the time the sharknose went on sale, 600,000 had been sold worldwide. So, if something vital appears to have been mislaid, or the condition is not perfect, you have no reason to waste the owner's time. Just walk away and find a better one.

Where to buy

A dealer will be able to offer you more protection in case that peach turns out to be a lemon. It will be more expensive, but Mazda has a pretty good approved used scheme with a decent warranty.

You still need to do your homework, however. It would be dangerous to assume that the salesperson will have an encyclopaedic knowledge of Mazda's back catalogue. So, for example, if you want power steering or other 'invisible' features, check out the details of the models with the owners' club or a book before you buy. Every dealer should have a reference book giving all the specifications and chassis numbers of every model and limited edition, so if you have any doubts about a car once you are at the showroom, you can suggest firmly that they dig it out.

The Vehicle Identification Number (VIN) at the back of the engine bay will record exactly which model it is. (James Mann)

Specialised dealers are another relatively safe option. Or there are auctions, but the best advice here is DON'T, unless you really know what you are doing.

You'll get more for your money if you buy privately, but be careful, there are some tatty cars out there. Again you'll need to read up about the model you are buying, and be on your guard in case that nice lady owner who left her son-in-law in charge of selling the car (shortly after losing all its documents) is off riding one of the pigs just flying past.

If you are buying a new MX-5 in the UK, then importing a UK-spec car from Europe, either independently or through a broker, could save you money. It's also worth getting a quote from a UK car broker who can buy cars in bulk and sell them at a discount. The best place to look quickly is on the internet, or in the buying and owning pages and advertisements of the monthly *What Car?* magazine.

Be sure of your car's history

Sadly, desirable sports cars like the MX-5 are irresistible to thieves; you only have to take a glance at the tear-jerking list of missing cars on the club website. You don't want to be one of the mugs buying these stolen cars – you could end up losing both the car and your cash.

Paperwork is vital, and the more of it the better – preferably strewn over a table in the seller's house with a mug of tea in your hand if you're buying privately, so you know the seller really lives there.

You need to know that the car really is what it is claimed to be, with all the right trim and options. In Europe, you also need to be sure a Mazda really is a Mazda and not a Eunos (see Chapter Eight.)

If you're answering a classified ad, always say you're calling about 'the car'. If the seller has to ask 'which one?', they could be a dealer or a thief.

When you're inspecting the car, make sure the vehicle identification number (VIN) at the back of the engine bay corresponds to the numbers of the registration documents and look to make sure there are no signs that it has been tampered with or replaced with a different plate.

It's always advisable to get a vehicle condition check when buying used, and if you are a member of a breakdown service, this will include a history check. If you don't go for the full check, you can also get a history check separately from HPI Equifax, Expirion, or *What Car?* History Check in the UK.

This will run your VIN against a number of registers held by the police, finance companies and the insurance industry to make sure it has not been reported as stolen or is an insurance write-off and that there is no outstanding finance on it. In the latter case you could lose the car because it still belongs to a finance company.

If it comes up as a write-off, your MX-5 could either be hiding accident damage, or worse it could be a 'ringer'. That is, it's a stolen car wearing the ID taken from a damaged vehicle.

A history check may turn up disturbing details which may also point towards an accident or a 'hot' car. For example, it may give the wrong colour or trim level, or perhaps it may have a record of the mileage which is strangely higher than the odometer says now. In this case it could also have been 'clocked'.

What to look out for

Bodywork
The Mazda doesn't suffer from a major rust problem. However, specialist Richard Ducommun of Maztek reports that he is just beginning to see early Mk1 cars suffering the creeping menace in the sill and chassis.

Some MX-5s will have been driven hard; look out for signs of rough treatment. (LAT)

(This is also a warning to owners of older cars to get them Waxoyled now!) The Mk1 can also suffer from aluminium corrosion on the bonnet and Mk1 headlamp covers, particularly in early cars, because the paint on these is thin and suffers badly from stone chips.

In fact, the paintwork on early cars can also be damaged by excessive polishing. Keen concours entrants have occasionally found themselves lovingly wiping a patch of primer. Later cars also have tougher paint.

Naturally, because they are driven with enthusiasm, MX-5s do frequently come into contact with the scenery, so make sure you view the car in good light – never in the rain. You'll need to look down the line of the car, check for uneven shutlines, bulging filler or poorly matched paintwork. Check carefully under the bonnet and beneath floormats, too, for signs of welding or overspray.

The Mk1's pop-up headlamps are very reliable,

Pop-up headlamps can suffer stone chips; if they are winking, the car has probably had a smash. (James Mann)

so if they're winking, your car may have suffered frontal damage. Plus, it's a good idea to clear any snow or ice off before raising them to avoid overloading the headlight motor. When you go to see a Mk1, raise and lower them a few times. If they are slow, it may be because they have not been used for a while, but it could also be an indication of damage.

You may decide you can live with minor scrapes if the price is right, but check hard for evidence of major damage which may ruin the way the car drives, or could even be dangerous.

If you are unfortunate enough to find yourself in a hedge, be aware that replacement panels can be quite pricey.

Colour can affect the price significantly. Red cars are always popular, the bronze, white and blue will be cheaper to buy, but harder to sell in the UK. A lot of early white cars were actually resprayed blue by their original dealer because they proved so difficult to shift.

Demand for different colours can change according to country or state. Generally, in sunnier climates brighter colours are more popular, but in colder, wetter places, bright yellow can stand out like a sore thumb. The Sunburst Yellow is always popular, but the owners' clubs reckon they are usually bought by the more out-going (and/or crazy) personalities among their members. White is popular in Japan because it is the national F1 racing colour, equivalent to British Racing Green. In the UK this is Crystal White, the Eunos Roadster is painted a prosaic Chaste White.

Hood

Although the hood is simple to erect and put down again, it can suffer from rough handling and will be expensive to replace. A large number of Mk1s have scratched, creased or even torn plastic rear windows. So put the hood up, check the plastic and the zip for fraying, loose threads or loose teeth. You can get the zip replaced by a hood specialist, but it can be quite a good bargaining tool. Hoods can also shrink and leak, so look for water damage on the doors and the sides of the windscreen.

Make sure the owner still has the tonneau cover, too. People frequently put this away in a cupboard to create more boot space, and then forget to replace it when they sell.

If it is at the back of a cupboard, this is also a good indication that they haven't been using it. So check the underside of the hood for fading or rain damage.

Hard-tops are interchangeable between the Mk1 and Mk2 and even between Mazda and Eunos, but the rubber seals will be different and can leak if they are not swapped for the correct items. The early versions, produced by TWR don't fit very well and do leak around the side windows. All hard-tops are now produced in Japan and fit much better. You can only buy them in the current colours, but you can have one resprayed.

Soft-tops are also interchangeable from Mk1 to Mk2, but some owners find the glass panel heavy and diffcult to manoeuvre while it is being zipped in and out, so this is not a popular swap.

If you put a Mk1 hard- or soft-top on to a Mk2 car, you will have to have a new section of wiring loom put in to link up with the heated glass window.

Interior

Cabins last very well, but check for cracked plastic, or wear on the outside of the seat which can be costly to fix. The early fabric was prone to bobbling (technical term 'pilling') so owners often consider retrimming them in leather. If the interior and pedal rubbers look worn and the clock has only recorded a low mileage, suspect 'clocking'.

Check all the electrical items such as power windows, lights and stereo to make sure they work as they should. The windows do close quite slowly, but they should raise and lower smoothly.

The central locking units of 1994-onwards 1.8iS models have been known to be 'lazy' and not lock the doors properly. The UK club thinks it has found the problem and a possible cure.

Air-conditioning is a very desirable option. It won't add to the price, but it will help you hook a buyer when it's time to make a change. Check that it works and give it a good blast regularly once you own the car to keep it in good nick. All air-con systems need recharging after five years, and corroded condensers in front of the radiator can prove costly.

As you open the door, have a look at the stainless steel kickplate to make sure that it has a protective strip underneath and that there is no rust bubbling up at either end. These kickplates were fitted to protect the sills from damage, but early examples had no protective strip and the metal-to-metal contact causes the paint to bubble up.

This is very localised and is surface not structural, but it looks tatty. The best solution is to have the plates removed, and the affected area treated and repainted. The new replacement plates have a strip of rubber

underneath to prevent the same thing occurring again. If the car still has warranty this should be carried out free of charge, or if you are buying from a dealer you could insist that this is done before you buy.

Engine

All MX-5 engines are strong and reliable and should pass six figures easily, in fact, the US Miata club recently held a competition to find the car with the most miles, and the winner had racked up 240,000.

Always test drive the car from cold. Look out for blue smoke in the exhaust, it means the car is burning oil. A happy engine will be quiet and clicking tappets indicate sloppy maintenance. Standard plug leads can fail, too, causing misfires.

The cambelt needs to be changed every 60,000 miles or five years and this job costs over £100. So make sure it has been done, and if it's coming up, haggle the price down to compensate.

Rust can bubble up at the end of the kickplate if there is no rubber strip underneath it. (James Mann)

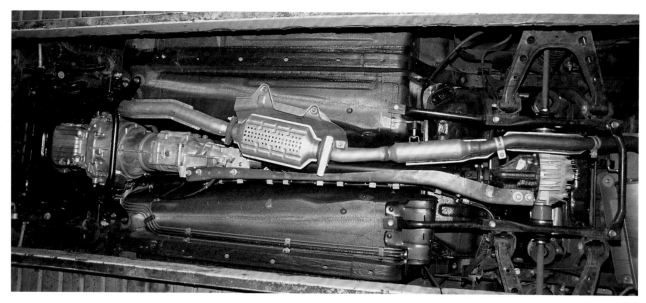

The catalytic converter may fail on older cars, and the exhaust heat shield can come loose and rattle. (LAT)

The catalytic converter has been known to fail on older cars and is very expensive to replace (around £350), so get an MoT or emissions certificate to make sure yours is working. The exhaust heat shield can also work loose and rattle, but this is not hard to fix.

Batteries last for years, but they are a special gel-filled unit and are expensive to replace. Mazda can fit a conventional battery by modifying the fixing brackets. If these are not modified and the battery is loose, it can short and cause a fire.

Gearbox

The gear lever should slide silently through the gate. Clunking or whining indicates there has been severe misuse.

Early cars up to K registration have a very notchy first-to-second gearchange. This is due to the use of a single-cone syncromesh on the second gear but has since been changed to dual cone to ease the problem. This notchiness should go away once the car has warmed up, so test drive the car long enough to make sure it does. Running synthetic gear oil is a good, but pricey solution if you can't live with it.

Most cars have a noisy clutch release bearing, but this should disappear when the clutch is depressed. If not, get it checked or negotiate a price reduction. Clutches also get squeaky if the car doesn't leave its garage very often.

High-mileage cars are likely to need a new clutch soon if they haven't already had one.

Wheels

The MX-5 has been fitted with an extraordinary number of different wheels, and not all are easy to replace, so make sure the car you are looking at has a perfect, unkerbed set. As well as looking awful, scuffed wheels don't say anything good about the driving or the attitude of previous owners.

All base models had steel wheels, the S models and limited editions had alloys, and some of these, such as the BBS wheels, do suffer from corrosion and pitting. Both the 10-spoke alloy of the 1992 Mk1 Black SE and the Mk2 10th Anniversary wheels were laquered to protect them, but the laquer was too thin and so corrosion gets started underneath. Most of the 10th Anniversary cars had their wheels replaced under

A scuffed wheel can be repaired, but may indicate a careless owner. (James Mann)

warranty, but the replacements will probably also suffer problems.

The standard Minilite-lookalike wheels are only laquered on the outside, so they can corrode on the inside. The best solution is to take them off, get rid of the powdery white corrosion with some wire wool and elbow grease and have some laquer put on by a wheel specialist.

Badly pitted and corroded wheels can also be sandblasted and refurbished by a specialist. Wicked Wheels in the UK has a mobile service to do this. You should knock the cost of this procedure off the purchase price.

While you're checking out the wheels, have a look at the brake discs too, because these can corrode and are quite pricey to replace.

Tyres
Check tyres for tread depth, and use as a bargaining point if you are going to have to replace them soon. MX-5's are generally gentle on tyres, so uneven wear may indicate steering or suspension damage.

Make sure the jack and tools are present and correct, and that the spare tyre has not been damaged.

Suspension
The major suspension parts should not need any major work, but if you buy a high-miler you may want to change the shocks and check the suspension bushes to keep the handling up to scratch.

Power steering
Manual steering is fine above around 20mph, but it does get heavy for low-speed manoeuvring and parking. Therefore power steering is a desirable option and although it won't necessarily add to the price of a car, it can make it easier to sell. Don't assume all limited editions will have power assistance; those based on entry-level models will not.

Which model?
Mk1
There are two quite different buyers for the Mk1, and what you have to look for depends to some extent on which one you are. If you want a cheap roadster, perhaps your first sports car, then a 10-year-old

The base-model 1.8i had plain steel wheels, wind-up windows and no power steering. (Mazda)

high-mileage MX-5 is an excellent choice. To keep the price down, you might have to put up with a few minor scrapes on the paintwork and fabric seats might be a little fluffy, but it is still guaranteed to be a reliable, everyday fun car.

If money is tight and you live in the UK, it's also worth considering a Eunos, which will offer just as much fun for less money.

On the other hand, the Mk1 is now officially a classic. After all, it has already adorned the front cover of *Classic & Sportscar* (June 2001). If you are buying

with this in mind, then your ideal car should be a low-mileage, early 1.6 in original condition.

Mk1 fans love the simpler, more retro shape, with those Elan-style pop-up headlamps and delightful details such as the chrome oval door handles inside and out.

Its fans will also tell you that the Mk1 is the best of the bunch to drive. The Mk1 also handles more like the roadsters of the Sixties, and for those who enjoy a bit of controlled oversteer, that's great. But it can catch out the unwary on damp or icy roads. In particular, drivers who have grown up at the wheel of an understeering

The Mazda badge changed to the more modern 'owl' for the Mk2. (James Mann)

The Mk1's chrome oval door handle is a beautiful piece of design, but the body-coloured Mk2 item snaps fewer fingernails. (James Mann)

hatchback, may find it disconcerting when the tail starts to twitch. The worst-case scenario on wet or icy roads is a pranged MX. Best advice is, buy the car, but take a skid course.

The early 1.6 delivers 114bhp and 100lb ft of torque, and its performance is very similar to the first 1.8 which replaced it. The rather coarse 1.8 unit, taken from the Mazda 323 GT also delivered 115bhp and it took a second longer to sprint to 60mph than the 1.6, although it overtakes the smaller-engined car at higher speeds. The 1.6 introduced in 1995 had been

The Mk1's outer chrome handle was echoed in black plastic inside the door; the modern theme continues inside the Mk2. (James Mann)

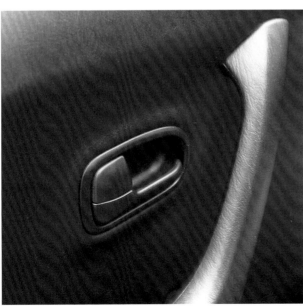

downgraded to 88bhp to differentiate it from the 1.8.

Mazda produced limited-edition models almost every year, and these vary in desirability; see below, but generally they fetch more than standard cars.

Mk2

There was a storm of protest when the Mk2 arrived in 1998, sans pop-up headlamps and a with a far more modern look. However fans have now grown to admire its slimmer lines and its slicker handling. Because it is newer, a Mk2 will probably have fewer miles on the clock and will hold its value better than an average-condition Mk1.

It is currently a good time to buy a Mk2 because it has just been replaced by the Mk3, and so second-hand values have taken a battering.

Mk3

The 'sharknose' slipped in surprisingly quietly, and its face-lift has been so subtle that some people are calling it a Mk2.5. So far, it has been received well by fans, who are pleased to see such details as white dials and touches of chrome in the cabin.

The turquoise blue of the first few cars is attractive, but will probably not hold its value as well as a good old classic red.

The variable valve-timing engine is more efficient from the point of view of emissions, but offers no significant performance advantage over the Mk2. It has a six-speed gearbox, or for the first time in the UK, a four-speed automatic is offered.

Which special edition?

Limited editions of all three generations are easier to sell on and, in the UK, are generally worth around £1,000 more than the cars on which they are based. With the rarer, or more popular editions it could be far more. But it is important to do your homework and know what you are buying. One strategy for shifting metal, popular with most volume manufacturers, is to give a basic-spec car a special badge and colour – and Mazda is not above this.

So don't assume a limited-edition car will have lots of electrical goodies and all the most up-to-date safety items of its time – they are frequently based on the lowest model in the range.

Where limited editions are based on the 1.8i, such as the Gleneagles, Harvard and Classic, Mazda often added power steering, but these models do without the rest of the S kit, including driver's airbag and electric mirrors. See Limited Editions for details.

The boot offers more useable space than before. The spare wheel and battery took up a large chunk of luggage space in the Mk1; these are stowed beneath the floor in the Mk2. (James Mann)

Opposite: The Mk2 appears to be a Mk1 that has toned its muscles in the gym, but both models have their ardent fans, and both hold their value very well. (Courtesy *Miata Magazine*)

Limited editions

Frequent limited editions were used in every market to boost sales and keep the product fresh, but most were produced locally, and bear little relation to one another. The only shared themes seem to be colours released at the same time because the Mazda factory turned out cars in batches of one colour and then dispersed them worldwide. For example, the UK British Racing Green Limited Edition and US Special Edition of 1991, the UK Merlot and US M edition, the 1998 Berkeley and Eunos VR Limited, both in Sparkle Green.

UK models

In the UK, the importer MCL bought cars from Mazda and was then allowed to enhance the cars or even respray them as the sales department thought fit. Additional novelties such as the Gleneagles' flat hat were sourced and added to increase desirability.

The cars chosen to be limited editions were frequently base models because it was more profitable to buy a a plain car in a good colour, dress it up with some alloy wheels and nice details then sell it for a higher price. This is a common sales tactic employed by most volume car manfacturers.

From 1990 until MCL lost the Mazda franchise in 2001, UK limited editions were built at its distribution centre at Sheerness. Mark Fryer still works at Sheerness, preparing new Kias. He remembers that he and his colleagues often threw in ideas to build a story or a character for a new special MX-5 based around a colour. The Monza was suggested after one employee had visited the Italian Grand Prix. A batch of rich red wine-coloured cars became the Merlot. Bright sunny yellow cars, evoking sun and sea escaped becoming the MX-5 Bognor and were christened California.

One of the first UK specials, produced around the same time as the first limited edition was the Le Mans.

Originally 24 were to be built, but a number of dealers recoiled in horror at the orange and green jester outfit, and after the first 10 had been slow to move, the run was cut short. Only 22 were ever completed. The final pair, which had had their BBR turbos fitted were sprayed a nice, safe black. Several more languished on dealer forecourts for a while before coming back for the same treatment. One, belonging to Clive Southern, had its green sprayed over orange by the dealer, and he bought it for a cut price. It is possible that only a handful still exist. One was restored from a very tatty wreck by UK club members Doug and Charlotte Nadin.

The most eleborate special was the Jasper Conran, created to make a car that stood out from an increasing tide of grey imports. Sadly, it missed the mark because it was selling for Mercedes money, and it is believed that MCL lost a great deal of money on the project. Again, some lucky owners got to snap up the most stubborn forecourt sitters for a song.

UK specials rated by the Owners' Club
BBR Turbo
Built: approx. 200
Rating: 10/10
Strictly speaking, the BBR Turbo was not a limited edition. As detailed in Chapter Three, this car was created for MCL in the UK by Brodie Brittain Racing. Kits were sold to and fitted by Mazda dealers and the entire car including the conversion was covered by the manufacturer's warranty. Usually painted red, black or white.

These cars are much sought after and rare – a number have been spotted in scrapyards, so fewer than the original 200 exist in the UK. Some kits were sold in the USA, but did not prove very popular and were soon withdrawn.

They are generally reliable, although exhaust manifolds tend to crack and cost around £400 to replace. A record of regular servicing and, in particular plenty of nice fresh oil, is even more essential. There have also been cases of leaks from the oil take-off pipe from the sump (the turbo uses the same oil as the engine) so look out for any signs of oil patches where the car has been parked.

Because the BBR is not a limited edition, it doesn't come with a numbered plaque, certificate or gifts. The conversion was only suitable for the Mk1 1.6.

1991 Mk1 Limited Edition

Built: 250
Rating: 9/10
Price new: £18,249
Celebrated the first birthday of the MX-5 in the UK. BRG, tan leather trim, leatherbound overmats, wood-rim wheel, gearknob and handbrake, deep pile carpet. Numbered dash plaque, leather wallet with matching plaque, certificate of authenticity. Embossed leather key fob.

Central locking, special console with distinctive clock, Clarion CRX111R radio-cassette with four

The BBR Turbo usually wore a rear spoiler; *Autocar*'s test car, driven against the Lotus Elan in 1991 didn't. (LAT)

The Limited Edition of 1991 had British Racing Green paint and its wire-lookalike alloys were painted green in between the spokes. (James Mann)

The Limited Edition had matching brass plaques displaying the car's individual number on the dash, and a leather wallet. (James Mann)

speakers, polished treadplates. Unique BBS alloys, 6Jx15 painted green inside, haven't been repeated since, so make sure you buy a car with a good set.

A chrome badge on the nose of this car is not an original feature.

The Mazdaspeed 787B was the first Japanese car to win Le Mans. MCL celebrated by creating the MX-5 Le Mans. (LAT)

1991 Le Mans

Built: 24
Rating: 10/10
Price new: £20,499

Produced to celebrate Mazda's victory with the quad-rotor 787B at the Le Mans 24-hour race, and wearing the same lurid green and orange paint scheme, plus plastic stick-on white tape. (*Motor Sport* described it as looking like a cross between a slice of Battenburg and an Argyll sock.) Underneath, the bonnet was the BBR turbo conversion, and it wore a ground-hugging body kit with a rear spoiler sourced from Finish Line.

It ran on OZ alloy wheels of 6J x 15 with a winner's laurel leaf and Le Mans 24 decals, and was well equipped, featuring power steering, electric windows, central locking and an alarm. The optional hard-top came in matching solid green. Each car came with a wallet including a card signed by the Le Mans-winning driver Johnny Herbert, who is perhaps better known in the UK for his Formula One career with Lotus, Benetton, Sauber, Stewart and Jaguar.

The official number made was 24, but actually, only 22 red cars were resprayed at MCL's Sheerness facility in the UK. At the time, they were extremely unpopular. One car, currently owned by UK club committee member Clive Southern, had the green squares resprayed orange by the dealer, so his car is unique.

The 1991 Le Mans limited edition MX-5 celebrated the famous win; Doug Nadin's car is very original. (Dougie Firth)

A Le Mans is masked up ready for addition of its Argyle-sock green diamond at Sheerness. (Mark Fryer)

Clive Southern's unique car had its green squares painted over by the dealer to make it more attractive! (Dougie Firth)

These cars were originally red before being resprayed in the UK. The engine was stripped out, but if you lift the carpets, the floor is still red.

April 1992–August 1993 SE
Built: 200
Rating 7/10
Price new: £18,686
Based on the 1.6i, and only available in Brilliant Black paint with SE badging. Ran on 10-spoke 7J x15 polished alloys with locking wheel nuts and low-profile 215/45/ZR15 tyres; ABS was standard. The cabin was trimmed with tan leather with a deep pile carpet, wooden steering wheel, gearknob and handbrake, stainless steel kick plates.

June 1993–February 1994 1.8i SE
Built: 150
Rating: 7/10
Price new: £18,449
As above, but with 6.5J x 15 wheels and now unpolished.

1994
Revised 130bhp 1.8 introduced.

May–October 1995 California
Built: 300
Rating: 8/10
Price new: £15,795
A very desirable model marking the fifth anniversary of the MX-5 in the UK. Based on the 1.8i, in Sunburst Yellow, it had power steering, immobiliser, but with manual windows, door mirrors and aerial. Five-spoke 7J x 15 alloys with 195/50VR 15 low-profile Dunlop tyres, Clarion CRX601R radio-cassette. California badge on back panel, number plaque and leather owner's wallet inside.

April 1995
1.6 reintroduced in addition to 1.8i and 1.8iS.

October 1995–May 96 Gleneagles 1.8i
Built: 400
Rating: 8/10
Price new: £16,995
Named after the famous Gleneagles Hotel and Golf Club near Stirling in Scotland. Based on 1.8i, with Montego Blue paint, black carpet and champagne leather seats and steering wheel. The tonneau cover was larger than usual, and tucks down just behind the seats. Impressive walnut-style wooden dash with hinged centre compartment, Gleneagles tartan trim on gear lever gaiter and a Gleneagles crest showing the eagle

The 1995 Sunburst Yellow California is one of most popular limited editions; only 300 were built. (LAT)

landing, on the centre of the steering wheel. Power steering, immobiliser, Clarion DRX8175R single-disc CD player, five-spoke 15in alloys. Gleneagles logos everywhere. The brochure read: 'The world-famous Gleneagles Hotel and Golf Club is steeped in tradition. These are values in common with the MX-5.'

The wood-effect console is actually just painted plastic, and the paint can fade or turn white if it has been in the sun or rain too much. Make sure you get the matching Tartan wallet. It originally came with a pair of tartan caps for the driver and passenger, but these are very rare, although you can buy a tartan golf cap from Gleneagles.

One example was raffled and the proceeds helped send Scottish athletes to the 1996 Olympics in Atlanta.

May 1996–January 1997 Monaco 1.6i
Built: 450
Rating: 5/10
Price new: £13,750
Based on 90bhp 1.6i with five-speed gearbox. Special British Racing Green paint, body-coloured mirrors,

The 1995 Gleneagles celebrated the famous golfing hotel; one example was raffled to help send Olympic Games competitors to Atlanta. (Simon Farnhell)

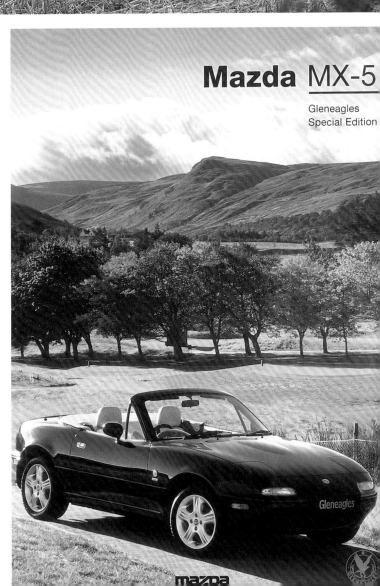

Mazda MX-5

Gleneagles
Special Edition

The 1996 Merlot limited editions were created around the batches of colours to be sent out by the factory. (Simon Farnhell)

Interior is very attractive, featuring grey leather, high-backed chairs with Merlot piping and wood inlay for the console. (LAT)

Monaco graphics and a contrasting tan hood. Reflex five-spoke alloy wheels with locking wheel nuts. Clarion ARB017E radio/cassette unit with removable front.

June–October 1996 Merlot 1.8i

Built: 600
Rating: 8/10
Price new: £16,350

Launched alongside the Monaco, but based on the 131bhp 1.8i with power steering. Vin Rouge mica paint with Merlot badging and matching mudflaps. Phantom five-spoke alloy wheels with locking wheel nuts, shod with Dunlop SP2000 tyres. Grey leather seats (US version had tan leather), wood dash trim. The first 400 had a leather-trimmed steering wheel, the final 200 made do with polyurethane. Clarion DRX8175R single-disc CD audio unit RDS/EON, immobiliser.

February–June 1997 Dakar

Built: 400
Rating 6/10
Price new: £17,210

A 1.8 with Twilight Blue metallic paint, colour-keyed door mirrors and rear mudflaps. Grey leather upholstery with dark blue piping and matching door panels. Burr walnut effect dash centre and console trims, chrome rear brace bar and treadplates. Momo leather-trimmed steering wheel. Dakar badging and floor mats, power steering, Sony XR C500 RDS radio-cassette, and immobiliser. Ran on 16-spoke 15in X 7JJ FOMB Activa alloy wheels with locking wheel nuts for security, on Dunlop SP Sport 2000 195/50VR15 tyres. Numbered plaque.

May–September 1997 Monza

Built: 800
Rating: 5/10
Price new: £14,595

Named after the famous Italian racetrack, the Monza wears British Racing Green with a Monza logo showing a map of the circuit and a laurel wreath on the nose and rear quarter panels. These plastic transfers have a habit of peeling off and no replacements are available.

It is based on the 1.6i, so in keeping with the racing

This Classic Black MX-5 was the winner of the UK Owners' Club 'Hot 5' concours 2001. It has a supercharged engine and body kit fitted by Maztek. (Andrew Priest)

cars that raced on the Monza banking, it has no power steering and the spec is very basic. It even has wind-up windows. It has five-spoke 14 x 6JJ Aliseo alloy wheels with locking wheel nuts and a Clarion AR6270 audio/cassette system.

May–September 1997 Harvard
Built: 500
Rating: 7/10
Price new: £17,495
Named after the famous US college (Oxford and Cambridge would have reminded UK buyers of some rather different cars). Based on the 1.8i, in Silver Stone metallic paint with Harvard badging and floormats. Five-spoke 15in x 7JJ Aliseo alloy wheels equipped with locking wheel nuts and 195/50 VR15 Pirelli P6000 tyres. Inside, the driver sat on sumptuous, burgundy leather upholstery with grey piping and held a Momo leather steering wheel while facing a dark burr wood dash.

Power steering, high power Clarion DRX8175R RDS audio/CD system, immobiliser, chromed brace bar, scuff plates. No ABS, airbags or power windows.

October 1997 Classic
Built: 400
Rating: 9/10
Based on the 1.8i, black paint, 15in alloys, black leather interior with red stitching, wood trim, Momo leather-rim steering wheel, power steering, stainless steel brace bar and scuff plates. RDS radio cassette, Classic key fob. No electric windows.

January 1998 Berkeley
Built: 400
Rating: 9/10
Price new: £17,600
The UK's final version of the Mk1 in Sparkle Green (turquoise) metallic paint, Berkeley decals on front wings below side flashers. Dark burr wood trim for console, leather seats with black facings and light grey centre, black leather gaiters on gear lever and

Newly imported Sparkle Green MX-5s are transformed into Berkeley limited editions at MCL's Sheerness PDI centre in 1998. (Mark Fryer)

handbrake, CD player, immobiliser. Stainless steel brace bar and scuff plates, plus chrome boot rack. Limited edition plaque and special Berkeley key fob. No ABS, airbags or power windows.

Mk2 limited editions

December 1998–1999 Sport 1.8i (Red)

Built: 300
Rating: 6/10
Price new: £22,535
Sadly the Sport really is no sportier than the standard 140bhp 1.8iS on which it is based. However, it wears a body kit with front fog lamps, available in red only and comes with a colour co-ordinated hard-top. Kit includes air-conditioning, a wood interior trim kit and seats with leather facings, and Sport carpet mats.

1999 Sport 1.8i (Blue)

Built: 300
Rating: 6/10
The demand for the Classic Red Sport was such, that it was followed by a version in Racing Blue.

The rare Mk2 10th Anniversary gift set included a pair of watches, a key ring and an exquisite model. (James Mann)

10th Anniversary

Built: 7,000 (3,700 for Europe, 600 for UK)
Rating: 10/10
The only limited edition to be offered worldwide, celebrated the MX-5's 10th birthday.

The UK Owners' Club Chairman, Allan Legg's 10th Anniversary has added foglamps and rear spoiler. (James Mann)

The Jasper Conran Platinum interior was plush Connolly leather, but the car was too expensive. (Mazda)

Based on the 1,8iS in Innocent Blue mica paint with highly polished wheels, Bilstein shocks from US 'sport package', power steering and, for the first time outside Japan, a six-speed close-ratio gearbox. The seats had black leather side panels and headrests with suede-look blue material on the centre panels. A Nardi leather-covered steering wheel and gear lever were also finished in black and blue. The speedo and rev counter had chrome surrounds and red needles.

The 10th Anniversary edition is much sought-after, but try to get one with good wheels. The laquer was notoriously thin, prompting a recall. Most were replaced, but the replacements often show similar problems, and new ones are rare.

Be sure to get your certificate and gifts which were a pair of Seiko watches with logo, and a model car. German dealers didn't always give them out, so now they're worth a fortune; the watches alone can fetch £200 each.

2000 Jasper Conran
Built: 500
Rating: 4/10

This special edition, based on the 1,8iS, featured interior enhancements care of fashion designer Jasper Conran. Of the 500 models produced, 100 were in Metallic Platinum with a red interior, and 400 were Classic Black with a black interior. Both had 15in BBS wheels and were trimmed inside with soft, aromatic Connolly hide as used by Rolls-Royce and Ferrari. Interior details included aluminium-effect fascia, gearknob and handbrake button. Entertainment came care of a Sony audio system with single CD and Minidisc changer. Each car was individually numbered and a donation for each car sold was given to the London Lighthouse. Price new was £21,000 for Classic Black, £24,000 for the Platinum which also came with a set of smart Jasper Conran luggage – and cost far too much for an MX-5, this edition selling like cold cakes.

The MCL press office takes an Andy Warhol approach to press packs. California, Divine and Isola. (Mazda)

2000 California Mk2

Built: 500
Rating: 5/10
Price new: £16,000

Once again in Sunburst Yellow with body-coloured mirrors. Based on the 1.6i with pretty much that model's standard equipment, twin airbags, air-con, power steering, a stereo radio-CD player, an immobiliser, and 15in alloys. Fans of the Mk1 California regard this car as a misuse of the name.

Mazda MX-5 California

Mazda MX-5 Divine

New Mazda MX-5 Isola

July 2000 Isola

Built: 500

Rating: 3/10

Price new: £16,000

Based on the MX-5 1.6i with five-speed gearbox; driver and passenger airbags, Isola badges, Classic Red with a hard-top, same 14in alloy wheels as California, 185/60/R14 82V Yokohama tyres. Audio fitment 'as per customer's choice' (in other words, none provided).

July 2000 Divine

Built: 500

Rating: 1/10

The what? The Divine was exactly the same as the Isola, but you had a stereo as standard instead of the

hard-top. In fact, the press office even sent out the same photograph with a different name on it.

You won't see many.

2000 Icon

Built: 750

Rating: 9/10

Price new: £19,200

Based on a 1.8iS, but with a six-speed gearbox. Art Vin (mahogony) mica paint, beige interior with leather seats and wood steering wheel, gearknob and handbrake handle. Cream dials with chrome rings and orange needle. Black roof with a tan tonneau in the UK, tan roof overseas.

The Icon was created in Japan, but its badges were sourced in the UK, and these tend to fall apart. At the moment it is still possible to get replacements, but they may become scarce.

Phoenix, the first Pan-European limited edition was the first Mk3 limited edition. (Mazda)

Mk3 limited edition

March 2002 Phoenix

Built: 1,200

Rating: tbc

Launched Europe-wide in both 1.6 and 1.8 guises. Came with a choice of black or titanium metallic grey with Sienna Brown leather heated seats and unique 15in alloy wheels. The Phoenix MX-5 SE 1.6i cost £15,995, the 1.8i £16,595 and the titanium paint added another £150. Equipment worth £1,600 was loaded on top, including remote door locking with boot release, electric mirrors, two-tone leather wheel, an electric aerial and two additional tweeters for the stereo, a Torsen limited-slip differential on the 1.8, and an aero board for the 1.6.

June 2002 Arizona

Built: 1000

Rating: tbc

This well-equipped new limited edition was launched for summer 2002. It was priced at £16,095 for the 1.6, or £16,605 for the 1.8; a premium of £1100 and £1200 respectively above the price of the standard cars. It came in Sunlight Silver, Blaze Yellow mica or Eternal Red, altough choosing one of the metallic colours would add another £250 to the price. Standard kit included unique 15in alloy wheels, style bars and windbreak, stainless steel scuff plates, aluminium centre console trim, remote central locking with boot release, electric windows, CD player and electric aerial. The heated seats were trimmed in black leather with silver stitching, as were the Nardi steering wheel, gear knob and handbrake lever. The 1.8 also had a Torsen limited-slip diff as standard.

US range

The rarest US specials are the 'color cars' given special paint in 1991 to test customer reaction to colours for the soon-to-be-tested MX-3. Each one is unique, and they are Orange, Teal Green metallic, Ice Green, Pale Yellow metallic, Electric Blue metallic and Raspberry metallic. The window sticker states, under Colour of your Miata, 'Various Test Colours'. All had an X for the colour code.

US options packages (dates introduced) 'color cars'

1989
Base model

Steel wheels, no audio system, manual steering.

Well equipped Arizona has style bars as standard. (Mazda)

A package

Power steering, leather-trimmed steering wheel, alloy wheels and stereo cassette.

B package

As above, but adding cruise control, headrest speakers. From 1992 an electric aerial was included and the optional hard-top was given a heated rear screen.

Colours were Classic Red, Crystal White or Mariner Blue; from Spring 1990 added Silver Stone metallic.

C package

Loaded with desirable features such as BBS alloy wheels, Nardi wood handles, stainless steel scuff plates, cruise control, headrest speakers and a power aerial. Brilliant Black only in 1992; from 1993 became available in all colours except Mariner Blue.

The brochure for US Special Edition in British Racing Green goes a little overboard with its Olde English theme. (Simon Farnhell)

R package

Built: 1,218 (not limited)

A pure sports option costing $1,500, launched at Chicago Auto Show 1994. Standard engine, but R package wears a body kit and rides on stiffer springs and bushes and firmer Bilstein shocks. Alloy wheels, Torsen limited-slip diff. Power steering and ABS were not available, the only options were air-con and a stripe designed by Mark Jordan. Handling was much sharper than standard car, but the ride bruised backsides.

Popular equipment package

Replaced A and B package from 1995, combining the features of both; adds Torsen diff from 1997.

1995 Leather package

Replaced C package with tan leather interior and tan vinyl top.

1996 Power steering package

Added power steering and wheel trim rings to standard cars. Montego Blue mica could now be specified on all cars in the range apart from R package.

1997 Touring package

Alloy wheels, power steering, leather steering wheel, electric windows, power door mirrors, door pockets.

US Special editions

1991 Special edition

Built: 4,000
Price new: $19,234

The first limited edition, in British Racing Green and playing on British roadster theme, but the equivalent of the Eunos V Special. Equipped with B package, tan interior and part-leather seats; Nardi wood gearknob, stainless steel scuff plates and CD player; brass plaque; Hard-top optional. Also available as an automatic at a slightly reduced premium. ABS brakes were also optional.

1992 Sunburst Yellow

Built: 1,500
Price new: $16,770

Only available with A package. Limited production, if not strictly a limited edition.

1993

Miata suspension revised, new badge.

1992 Black Miata

Built: 4,626 (not limited)
Price new: $18,800

Initially classed as a C package option. Brilliant Black exterior, tan leather interior with matching hood; BBS 14in alloy wheels. At this point, it was the only Miata to be offered with the C package. A hard-top, automatic, ABS, air-conditioning, CD player and limited-slip differential were all optional.

1993 Limited edition

Built: 1,500 limited edition
Price new: $22,270

Brilliant Black model wears front and rear spoilers with BBS alloy wheels on 185/60 R14 tyres. Red interior and red vinyl tonneau. Leather steering wheel, Nardi leather gearknob, MSSS stereo system, stainless steel treadplates and speaker grilles, special key fob and Miata book. It rode on Sports suspension which includes Bilstein shocks and revised springs. All A and B package options included, plus limited-slip diff and anti-lock brakes standard.

1.8 replaces 1.6.

1994 M edition
Built: 3,000
Price new $21,645
Introduced alongside R package. Luxury model in Montego Blue mica with tan leather interior and tan hood. Nardi wooden gearknob and handbrake handle, electric windows and mirrors, cruise control, central locking and special key fob. Highly polished seven-spoke alloy wheels. Torsen diff was standard. Hard-top, ABS and automatic were optional, but ABS came as standard equipment with the auto.

1994 and 1995 Laguna Blue and Tan
Built: 463
Price new: 1994 $20,155; 1995 $20,925
This was actually a standard C package Miata, but it is regarded as a special model by many enthusiasts. Air-con, hard-top, ABS, Premium Sound System, automatic transmission, all optional.

1995 M edition
Built: 3,500
Price new: $23,980
One of the most sought-after Miatas. Rich Merlot mica paintwork, 6J x 15in BBS alloys fitted with 195/55 tyres. ABS, limited-slip diff. Leather interior trim, Nardi wooden gearknob and handbrake trim, polished kickplates, M edition mats, air-conditioning, CD player and four speakers, M edition key fob and lapel pin.

1996
133bhp engine introduced, MSSS now known as Mazda Premium Sound System.

1996 M edition
Built: 2,968
Price new: $25,210
Limited to four-month production run; Starlight mica paint from Millenia saloon, 15in Enkei five-spoke alloys. Tan leather seats with matching tan hood and hood cover, leather-trimmed steering wheel, Nardi

wooden gearknob and handbrake handle. High level of equipment including power windows and mirrors. Blue Miata logo on seatbacks, M Edition logo on tachometer and exterior M Edition badge. Automatic gearbox and hard-top optional.

1997 M edition
Built: 3,000
Price new: $24,935
Marina Green mica, tan leather trim and hood; highly polished six-spoke 15in alloy wheels, stainless steel kickplates, special floormats, Nardi wooden gearknob and handbrake handle and air-conditioning. Premium Sound System with CD player and headrest speakers. M edition logos on seatbacks and tachometer, M edition pen/key lapel pin. Included Popular equipment package. Torsen limited-slip differential, rear subframe brace.

1997 STO
Built: 1,500
Price new: $22,970
STO stands for Special Touring Option – or, according to its many fans: Still The One. Twilight Blue mica, wearing a rear spoiler, tan leather interior and tan vinyl top, 15in Enkei five-spoke alloy wheels and low-profile 50-series tyres, Stainless steel scuff plates, CD player, Nardi gear lever knob, STO insignias on the interior and floormats. Automatic and air-conditioning optional. List of features not available included cruise control, ABS, Torsen diff, Premium Sound System, electrc antenna or factory hard-top.

1999 10th Anniversary
Built: 7,500 (3,150 to USA, 3,700 to Europe, 500 to Japan, remainder to Australia and New Zealand)
Sapphire Blue mica, highly polished alloy wheels, black and blue leather-trimmed Nardi steering wheel, blue suede seats, six-speed gearbox. Bose stereo system.

2000 Mahogony mica
Very popular limited edition with a six-speed gearbox from the 10th Anniversary edition, cream interior, white dials with chrome trim rings, chrome door handles, stainless steel scuff plates and unique keys with cream head covers.

2001 Special Edition
Built: 3,000
Price new: $26,195
Celebrating the 10th anniversary of the first Special

The 10th Anniversary MX-5 had blue and black leather-trimmed interior and six-speed gearbox. It is the only limited edition to have been offered worldwide. (Mazda)

edition, the 2001 version also has British Racing Green paintwork with a Nardi wood-rimmed steering wheel and polished wood gearknob. The list of standard features includes air-conditioning, power windows, mirrors and locks, fog lights, cruise control, and chromed 16in alloy wheels. Other Special edition features are a British Racing Green Miata gift set, Special edition floor mats, stainless steel scuff plates, tan leather upholstery and a tan convertible top. ABS and hard-top are optional.

2002 Special Edition
Built: 2,500
Price new: $21,280
Available in two colour combinations: 1,500 in Titanium Gray metallic with Saddle Brown interior and 1,000 in Blazing Yellow mica with (for the first time) Classic Black leather seats with silver stitching, black dash and trim. Both cars have a six-speed transmission as standard. The body wears SE badges, a chrome-plated aluminium fuel filler cap, the wheels are new 16in alloys. Inside the cabins, the driver grips a Nardi steering wheel and is surrounded by aluminium-style details including vent rings, and a leather handbrake

handle with a silver release button. Entertainment is provided by a Bose AM/FM six-disc CD changer.

Colours
Classic Red 1990+
Silver Stone metallic 1990–92
Crystal White 1990–93
Mariner Blue 1990–93
British Racing Green 1991
Brilliant Black 1992+
Sunburst Yellow 1992
Laguna Blue metallic 1994–95
White 1994–97
Montego Blue mica 1994–97
Merlot mica 1995
Starlight mica 1996
Marina Green mica 1997
Twilight Blue mica 1997
Sapphire Blue mica 1999
Pure White 1999–2001
Emerald mica 1999+
Highlight Silver metallic 1999+
Evolution Orange mica 2000
Mahogony mica 2000
Crystal Blue metallic 2001
Midnight Blue 2001
Sunlight Silver 2001

Chapter **Eight**

The Eunos Roadster

The British and the Japanese have one very important thing in common: their cars have their steering wheels on the right. However, where the Japanese like to impress their neighbours with shiny, brand-new cars, the Brits like to be seen to be smart with money, and will happily boast that they bought all their Christmas cards in the January sale the year before.

For the bargain-hungry British, a car that is almost exactly the same but cheaper because it wears a different badge, is irresistible. So used Eunos Roadsters, discarded by the Japanese, are highly sought after in the UK, and are frequently imported via Ireland. The prices of Japanese cars plummet after they are three years old because of the draconian 'shaken' inspection, the name of which describes how the owner feels once he's paid the fee of £600 to £1,000. So it is possible for the Roadster to be bought, shipped over and still be sold for less than a second-hand Mazda MX-5.

Plenty of Roadsters also find their way to Australia and New Zealand which share a preference for driving on the left, and which received fewer 'official' MX-5s than the UK. The MX-5 Club New Zealand reports on its website that around 80 per cent of its members own a Eunos. However, in Australia these cars usually end up on the racetrack because of the continent's strict design rules governing road cars.

The Eunos name was used in Japan to create a separate brand from Mazda's family fare, in the same way Lexus is used by Toyota in the UK and USA. It was dropped from the Mk2 onwards (known in Japan as the MBA), but few such new Japanese cars have made it to the UK.

The Roadster tends to be better equipped than its European counterpart, offering standard luxuries such as air-conditioning and headrest speakers, electric windows and leather seats, a fact also appreciated by

enthusiastic British owners. It also had a quite different series of limited editions and frequently sported different suspension set-ups. However, in most respects the MX-5 and Roadster are mechanically identical.

Naturally, the official Mazda line tends to stress the differences and difficulties of owning a Roadster, and the company has been fighting 'grey' imports since before the UK launch in 1990. There are now so many Roadsters in the UK, that a thriving specialist network has appeared to support owners. They are still cheap, too, and so well worth a look.

The Eunos is labelled a 'grey' import, as opposed to a UK-spec MX-5 imported from Europe which is known

It seems a little unkind to label the original Mk1 Roadster as the Joker; perhaps it means they're more fun? (Andrew Fearon)

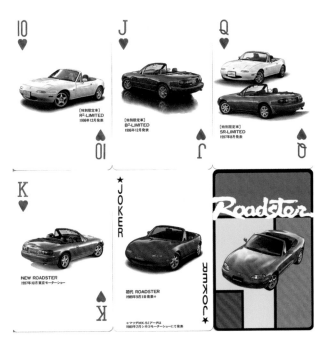

From the front, the only visible difference between the Mk1 MX-5 and Eunos Roadster is the badge. (LAT)

as a parallel import. When they first started appearing in the UK, the Roadsters were unpopular because they brought down the residual values of the existing MX-5s. However, this has settled down now; the Roadster is accepted on equal terms by the UK Owners' Club and around a third of the members now own them. This is vital for Roadster owners because insurance companies are often reluctant to cover grey imports, not knowing enough about them to be able to quote a realistic premium price. However the club now offers insurance on an equal footing with UK cars.

Servicing should not be a problem, as most items used are identical, although because Roadsters have standard air-conditioning, the 60,000-mile service will be more expensive to cover the changing of a slightly different drive belt. It will only cost the same as a service for a Mazda fitted with optional air-con though.

So, if anyone warns you that when they plug in the diagnostic machine it won't be able to read what's going on because the instructions come up in Japanese, say: 'Oh yes,' and 'you once picked up a hitch-hiker who disappeared'. It's nonsense.

It is true that the Eunos had a catalytic converter from launch, whereas the UK car only had one from 1992, and it has a different ECU (engine management system) which makes the engine run leaner to pass stricter Japanese smog regulations. Together, these emissions-reducing items will slightly reduce the performance of the car. The ECU rarely fails, but if it does, a specialist can order one from Japan very easily.

If the manager of your local service department sucks his teeth, shakes his head and gives the impression servicing your car is going to be a problem, then shop around and find one of the many helpful dealers who are more than happy to take your money. Mazda dealers are all franchisees, so their attitudes towards Roadsters do vary. Or you can visit one of the many specialists importing and servicing cars or providing spares.

Most spares are readily available new or secondhand. The only hitch is if you need a specific spare which is not in stock. Because the Mazda and Eunos have so many limited editions, all with different trim and suspension set-ups, your dealer or specialist will have to run a search to get the correct part number before it can be ordered. This search through the central computers can sometimes take weeks.

Even if you decide you don't want a Eunos, it's a good idea to be aware of the main differences between the Roadster and the MX-5, because some unscrupulous sellers have been known to switch badges and sell cars for higher prices. Some will also put a badge from a UK limited edition such as a California or a Merlot on a Eunos of the appropriate colour, even though the Roadster special editions were quite different. If you were caught out by either of these cons, you would still have a great car, but you'd have paid too much for it, and you'd lose out again when you came to sell it on.

Eunos in the UK

Most of the cars to be imported are early 114bhp 1.6 models, but they often have a very low mileage for cars of their age, frequently recording just 5–8,000km (3–5,000 miles) per year. As with the MX-5, original, standard cars are sought-after, but available only in small numbers.

By far the most plentiful model is the V Special, manual or automatic, with its tan leather and wood package. The S Special is also around in quite large numbers and is a more desirable option.

Other limited editions, such as the RS have also reached these shores. However, specialists have spotted some oddities, such as a silver car with V Special options (it was never available in this colour, see details of special editions below).

The Eunos badge is quite distinct from the Mazda items (See Chapter Six). (James Mann)

The Japanese like to personalise their cars and spend plenty of cash modifying their Roadsters. So at least 80 per cent of the cars shipped over have some sort of mod, be it a simple strut brace, some added chrome or a truly appalling body kit.

The standard of workmanship demonstrated by Japanese modifying companies tends to be high, but obviously the mods themselves are a matter of taste.

DID YOU KNOW?

Japanese cars are 'shaken' not stirred

Japanese cars must pass a regular rigorous inspection and repair procedure, carried out by a government inspection station on behalf of the Japanese Ministry of Transport.

After three years a car must undergo a 'shaken', which is a combination of inspection and minimal mandatory liability insurance. The next is at six years old, then eight, then 10. After 10 years, a new shaken is required every year. If the inspector demands new brakes, exhaust or other items, the shaken can cost £600 to £1,000.

Eunos Roadsters usually wear an inspection sticker in the top corner of their windscreen to show when they were last inspected. They should also have plenty of stickers under the bonnet. If one doesn't, it may have had its bonnet replaced following an accident.

Eunos Roadsters display Japanese Ministry of Transportation stickers to show they have passed regular rigorous inspections. The 9 refers to the 9th year of the current Emperor (1999). (James Mann)

A good support network has sprung up to cater for owners of imported Roadsters; they are also welcome in the UK Owners' Club. (James Mann)

The Eunos steering wheel is on the right and cabins tend to be better equipped than the UK MX-5. (James Mann)

Watch out if the wheels have been changed, though, because they could ruin your Roadster's deliciously balanced handling. Some of those fitted with suspension kits using Bilstein shock absorbers have an uncomfortably hard ride, too.

One serious concern is that a large number of Japanese sports cars, including Roadsters, are stolen in Japan and shipped abroad. A new service has been set up to check a potential buy through franchised dealers of Japanese cars using the VIN (Vehicle Identification Number). BIMTA (British Independent Motor Trade Association www.bimta.co.org) will also check the stolen-vehicle register and run a mileage check. In either case, there is a small fee. If the car is stolen, the details will be passed on to the nearest police Stolen Vehicle Squad. However, if you already own the car, it may still be possible to negotiate legal title to it.

Spotting a Eunos

Apart from the badge on the nose, the most obvious difference is the back panel, which has a square indentation for the number plate, rather than the MX-5's rectangle. The side flashers will be red rather than amber. Looking inside the cabin, if an early car has air-conditioning, headrest speakers or an automatic transmission (only available on the MX-5 from the Mk3) then it's a Eunos. Some later models do not have airbags where the UK equivalent would.

The best way to make sure your 'Mazda' is not a dressed up Eunos, however, is to check the VIN number at the back of the engine bay. Genuine MX chassis

IMPORTING A EUNOS FROM IRELAND

If you're feeling adventurous and you'd like to save even more money, you can travel to Ireland and pick up a Eunos from a dealer or an auction there.

You will need a file of paperwork and some patience to make sure you have every last piece of red tape tied in a bow.

Make sure you have: A ZZ temporary registration in Ireland to allow you to drive the car back from there

Proof of travel to Ireland (tickets)

Bill of sale from vendor

Valid UK insurance note

UK MoT (using chassis number as ID)

V55/5 application for first licence

V875 declaration of personal import

Japanese logbook with English translation

Japanese certificate of cancelled registration

SAD2 Euro customs declaration stamped with SAD ISO number, verification of customs duty paid

Once back in the UK, you will need to make copies of all documents, then take the bundle of originals to your local Vehicle Registration Office (not the Post Office) together with a cheque for a road fund licence and registration fee (this is currently £25).

Your tax disc will be sent by post, followed by your V5 (logbook). Most of the paperwork will be sent back eventually, but the DVLA will keep the Japanese documents.

numbers start with JMZ and have 13 characters, the Eunos chassis numbers begin NA. All UK Mazdas are also listed at Mazda UK, so you can call to check on Tel. 0845 6013 147.

Naturally, any handbook that comes with the car will also be in Japanese, but English versions are available from specialists.

Around 15 per cent of all Japanese Roadsters were automatic, but this option was not offered in the UK until the current Mk3 car. Automatics are extremely unpopular in the UK. All Roadsters have an airbag from 1996 onwards.

A large number of imported cars have been modified. This brochure shows just a few of the performance parts on offer to Japanese buyers. (Simon Farnhell)

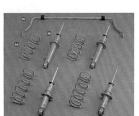

Conversion to UK spec

Any car up to 10 years old which is imported into the UK will need to pass a Single Vehicle Approval test costing £180. This is a tough test which makes sure the car meets British safety standards, and to pass it, cars must be fitted with items such as European-spec tyres and foglamps and a speedo in mph rather than kph. The Roadster can also fail if its vent and heater knobs protrude too far, so causing a risk of injury in an accident. (These can be changed.)

A small restricter should also be slipped into the Japanese car's wider fuel opening, to make sure it can only take an unleaded fuel nozzle.

On top of this, it will have to have an MoT test if the car is over three years old. A specialist dealer should have carried out these tests, so ask to see the paperwork.

The chrome rings around the dials often snap when the dial faces are changed, but reproductions are easily available. The standard radios have a different range of frequencies making it impossible to pick up some UK stations. Radio-band expanders can be fitted to the standard Panasonic unit to allow you to receive the

majority of UK stations, or some people prefer to fit a new stereo. If the central console around the radio cracks while your fab new ICE is being fitted, don't kill the fitter, it happens a lot, and a replacement section is available.

Does the Eunos suffer any particular problems?

Because Japan has a kinder climate than the soggy, wet UK, the Eunos is not as well protected as the Mazda against rust. It's vital, therefore, to get your Roadster undersealed, and preferably Waxoyled. Particularly vulnerable areas are the rear section behind the seats and the boot.

Many cars arrive in the UK without a service history or verification of the mileage, so it's hard to know whether it has been well looked after. Even the age of your car may be a mystery, although you can probably find it on a sticker; check out the seat base, the white label on the door post or the label at the base of its seatbelt webbing. Some dealers will be able to offer a warranty, usually a mechanical beakdown insurance rather than the cover offered on a new car.

The Eunos is just as reliable and robust as its Mazda brother, but it's a good idea to give it an oil service immediately, if the importer has not already done so. Oil pressure should be 1.8–6.0kg/cm. It should run at

The major difference between the Roadster and MX-5 is the shape of the recess for the rear number plate (the later car also has a boot-mounted rear brakelight). (James Mann)

USEFUL CONTACTS

Abbotts Paint and Body Ltd
Copthorne Bank, Copthorne, West Sussex RH10 3JF
Tel: 0780 495 345
Specialists in paint and body repairs to MX-5 and Eunos Roadsters.

Cox & Buckles Workshop
Elm Grove, Wimbledon, UK
Tel: 020 8944 7100
www.cox-and-buckles-workshop
All MX-5 and Eunos servicing and mechanical work, bodywork. Dealer-beating prices, work carried out by ex-Moss garage mechanics.

Culcheth Car Spares
457a Warrington Road
Culcheth, Cheshire WA3 5SJ
Tel: 01925 762279
Number plates for Eunos 13in x 6.5in, £15 a pair (at time of publication).

Eunosverse
Eunosverse, PO Box 124 Oxted RH8 OGA
Tel: 0800 026 5594
www.eunosverse.com
Parts and accessories for MX-5 and Eunos Roadster.

Euro-spec 2000 Ltd
Tel: 01276 670628, fax 01276 670638
e-mail: Eurominx@aol.co
Specialises in SVA and MoT test conversion work, spares, bulbs, undersealing on most vehicles. Can arrange imports through an agent.

Sam Goodwin at Bedworth
King St, Bedworth, Nuneaton, Warwickshire CV12 8JE
Tel: 02476 313909
www.samgoodwin.com
e-mail: sam@samgoodwin.com
Eunos specialist: imports, parts and service, hoods.

Ka Yu Auto Parts
3 Black Bank, Exhall, Coventry CV7 9NX UK
Tel: 02476 318729
www.kayuautos.com
e-mail: kayuautos@msn.com
Parts and accessories for Mazda and Eunos.

Les's Roadster Pages
Accessed through a link on Mike Heyward's website or on www.home.clara.net/nardn/japmot.htm
Shows Japanese stickers eg Japanese Ministry of Transportation inspection stickers (similar to an MoT certificate).

2.0kg/cm at tickover when warm, or drop to 1.8 when the engine is hot.

Fit a new set of HT leads while you're at it. In common with the MX-5, these can fail after about 20,000 miles, and the catalytic converter can be damaged if the car runs too long with faulty leads.

The car should accelerate and slow down smoothly, so any hesitation may indicate faulty leads. Check that the cat light on the dash goes out when you start the car, to make sure you're not too late.

Some 1989–90 cars suffer from a crankshaft problem which causes the car to cut out, or accelerate sluggishly, but this is rare.

Power-window motors seem to burn out or fail frequently, in common with the Mazda.

Most Roadsters have headrest speakers as standard as well as speakers in the doors. Many of these were incorrectly wired and sound very thin. See website www.Miata.net archives for a solution.

Check the tyres carefully, as you would on any older car. The Japanese tyres are made of a hard compound rubber and have a tendency to crack, particularly on the outer edges. If the car has been through an SVA, they may have been swapped already. Otherwise budget for a new set of Yokohama A509s or A520s.

The plastic rear windows of cars in the hotter areas of Japan tend to go brown and crack, especially if careless owners have not bothered to unzip the window or fit the tonneau cover while the roof is down. Again, this is problem shared, although to a lesser extent, by older Mazdas.

A number of owners have expressed concern about regulations introduced in September 2001, which specify a precise size and spacing for registration numbers. In fact, this should not affect the Eunos. The DVLA reassures us that the number can still go over two lines to fit into the car's square rear recess, as long as the numbers and letters themselves conform to the correct size and spacing.

The plate itself is an odd size, but Culcheth Car Spares near Warrington offers them for a small price (Tel. 01925 762279).

EUNOS RANGE

September 1989
Date introduced.

Standard 1.6i
Steel wheels, three-spoke Eunos steering wheel, manual steering, not very popular in Japan and quite rare in UK.

1.6 Special package Adds power steering, seven-spoke alloy wheels, electric windows, leather trimmed Momo steering wheel. The Special package was always a popular option, accounting for almost half of all sales.

Optional extras: automatic transmission (n/a on base models from 1991), limited-slip differential, uprated suspension, Mazdaspeed five-spoke 6J x 14in, SPA 17-spoke 6J x 14in wheels, polished cam cover, chromed door mirrors, front spoiler, air-conditioning, CD player, polished kickplates, alloy handbrake grip, wood trim package.
   Colours available: Crystal White, Classic Red, Mariner Blue, Silver Stone metallic.
   Extra brace bar was added to rear suspension after July 1991.

1990 V Special
Available as a manual or automatic. Neo Green, tan leather with matching hood cover, wood package with Nardi steering wheel, power steering, air-conditioning, power windows, CD player. Polished kickplates added by door speakers. From 1993 had the Sensory sound system as standard. Gains Nardi steering wheel from 1995. The most common Eunos model in the UK. May have BBS wheels.

Optional extras: air-conditioning, hard-top, limited slip diff, CD player, chrome door mirrors, polished treadplates, fog lamps, Auto.

1991 V Special
Also available in Brilliant Black, polished kickplates added.

Side impact bars and option of an airbag added July 1992.

August 1992 S Special
Price new: 220,000 yen
Sporty model in Classic Red or Brilliant Black with a rear spoiler. Manual only. Chassis stiffened with front strut brace, Bilstein dampers and BBS 6J x 14 alloy wheels with 185/60 tyres. Nardi three-spoke leather-trimmed wheel, gearknob. Mazda Sensory Sound Stereo (MSSS). Stainless steel kickplates and speaker grilles.

1993
1.8 replaces 1.6, chassis stiffened as for MX-5 and Miata. Model line-up as above continues; entry-level 1.8 has basic equipment as 1.6i above. Auto only available on Special Package and V Special.

V Special Type II
Price new: 2,486,000 yen
Adds a tan hood, chrome door mirrors and a set of highly polished seven-spoke alloy wheels to the existing V Special package. Nardi three-spoke steering wheel from 1995.

S Special
Price new: 2,111,000 yen
Now either Brilliant Black or Laguna Blue with Special equipment spec including uprated suspension with Bilstein shocks and thicker anti-roll bars, a front tower brace, a rear body brace, 14in BBS alloy wheels, Nardi steering wheel, polished kickplates and speaker surrounds, as above. Manual only.

1993/94
1.8 model introduced with extra chassis stiffening, Torsen differential added as Mazda MX-5 models.

1994
Brilliant Black added to basic colour line-up. S Special now also offered in Chaste White.
   Spec changes 1995/96 include 133bhp engine, lightened flywheel, 4.3:1 final drive, standard airbag, rear-view mirror light. Roadster script on rear changes from red to green.

1995
M package takes Roadster line-up to seven. Steel wheels, three-spoke steering wheel, but power-assisted steering, electric windows and better stereo.

Special package can now be specified as manual or automatic, plus limited-slip differential with the manual version. Equipment as above: power steering, seven-spoke alloy wheels, electric windows, leather-trimmed Momo steering wheel; adds power mirrors, driver's airbag and improved stereo system.

S Special Type II adds 6J x 15 BBS alloys on low-profile Bridgestone Potenza RE010 tyres.

1996
All models adopted new Momo four-spoke steering wheel with airbag.

1998
Mk2 1.6 and 1.8 launched; Eunos becomes Mazda.

1.6

Standard package Manual steering, manual windows, Mazda four-spoke steering wheel, five-speed gearbox, steel wheels.

Colours available: Chaste White, Classic Red, Highlight Silver metallic.

M package Power steering, electric windows, Mazda four-spoke steering wheel, stereo; Torsen differential, steel wheels.

Colours: Chaste White, Classic Red, Highlight Silver metallic, Twilight Blue mica, Brilliant Black.

1.8

M package power steering, electric windows, base steering wheel, stereo and six-speed gearbox.

Special package Power steering, electric windows, electric door mirrors, Momo leather steering wheel with airbag, six-speed gearbox, Torsen differential, anti-lock brakes.

S Special Six-speed gearbox, Nardi leather steering wheel and gearknob, five-spoke alloy wheels.

RS Special Six-speed gearbox, Torsen differential, 15in wheels, Nardi leather steering wheel and gearknob.

VS Special Grey Green mica, tan leather trim, Nardi wood-

A Japanese brochure showing RS and VS Specials; both had six-speed gearboxes, Nardi wood steering wheels and leather trim. (Simon Farnhell)

rimmed steering wheel, gearknob and handbrake lever, CD player; six-speed gearbox.

10th Anniversary As UK and US (offered worldwide).

Optional extras – automatic transmission, anti-lock brakes, air-conditioning, hard-top, limited-slip differential, CD player.

Roadster limited editions

August 1991 J Limited
Built: 800
Price new: 1,900,000 yen
Based on Special package. Sunburst Yellow paint; wood trim package for interior plus stainless steel kickplate. Optional hard-top. Auto available for an extra 40,000 yen. Entire 800 allocation was sold within the first day.

December 1992 S Limited
Built: 1,000
Price new: 2,350,000 yen
Based on S Special. Brilliant Black with gold-coloured BBS alloy wheels; red leather interior and Sensory Sound System.

November 1993 Tokyo Limited

Built: 40

Price new: manual 2,458,000; automatic 2,508,000 (the M2-1002 was 3,000,000 yen)

Brilliant Black with gold BBS alloy wheels and tan hood. Used high-quality interior parts left over from the unsuccessful M2-1002 including cream leather interior and trim details and (see Chapter Three) Sensory Sound System.

December 1993 J Limited II

Built: 800

Price new: manual 2,030,000 yen; auto 2,080,000 yen

Based on the Special package, in Sunburst Yellow with a black windscreen surround. Bucket seats with separate headrests, high-power audio system with CD player. Available as manual or automatic. 6J x 14in seven-spoke alloy wheels with Pirelli P700-Z tyres.

July 1994 RS Limited

Built: 500

Price new: 2,215,000 yen

Sporty Roadster based on S Special. Standard 1.8 engine, with lightened flywheel and lower 4.3:1 final drive. Montego Blue mica paint with RS decals on front wings. BBS wheels with Bridgestone Potenza RE010 P195/55 HR15 tyres. Recaro bucket seats, Nardi leather-rimmed three-spoke steering wheel.

January 1995 G Limited

Built: 1,500

Price new: manual, 1,900,000 yen

Based on M package, available with manual or automatic transmission. Satellite Blue mica paint and dark blue hood with seven-spoke alloy wheels. Low-back bucket seats as used for the J Limited II. Momo leather steering wheel, uprated audio system.

February 1995 R Limited

Built: 1,000

Price new: 2,175,000 yen

Like RS Limited, this sporty model had a lightened flywheel and 4.3:1 final drive ratio. Satellite Blue mica (894) or Chaste White (106) with a blue hood and 15in BBS alloys on Bridgestone Potenza tyres. The interior was trimmed in red leather with a three-piece wood trim package.

December 1995 VR Limited

Built: 1,500

Price new: 2,080,000 yen

Available in two guises, both based on the S Special Type I:

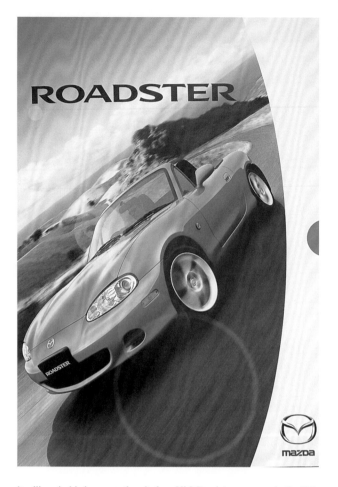

It will probably be some time before Mk3 Roadsters appear in the UK. (Simon Farnhell)

Combination A (700) Vin Rouge mica paint with tan hood and matching leather trim, alloy gearknob, shift plate and handbrake lever. Five-spoke 6J x 15in alloys.

Combination B (800) Excellent Green mica with dark green hood, black leather upholstery, alloy gearknob and handbrake handle as Combination A, plus five-spoke alloy wheels. Five-spoke 6J x 15in alloys.

December 1996 B2 Limited

Built: 1000

B2 stood for Blue and Bright; as the Twilight Blue mica bodywork and dark blue hood were complemented by polished seven-spoke, 14in alloy wheels, chrome mirrors and dial surrounds shone from the dash. The buckets seats were trimmed in black moquette, a CD player was standard and air-conditioning optional.

R2 Limited

Built: 500

Launched at the same time as the B2, the R2 stood for Racy and Red, although only the interior was red with black trimmings, the bodywork being painted Chaste White. Five-spoke, 6J x 15 alloy wheels wore Bridgestone Potenza tyres. Equipment based on the S Special Type I; alloy gearknob, shift plate and handbrake grip, chromed dial surrounds.

The M2 1008, created by the short-lived Japanese M2 division, is a rare beast unlikely to be seen on these shores, see Chapter Three. (Simon Farnhell)

August 1997 SR Limited

Built: 700

Price new: 1,978,000 yen

The SR celebrated the eighth birthday of the Roadster. Based on the M package, either manual with Torsen differential or automatic transmission. Sparkle Green (316) or Chaste White (384) with highly polished seven-spoke alloy wheels and chromed mirrors. Black leather upholstery with light grey nubuck-type inserts, chromed dial rims, Momo steering wheel, Nardi gearknob, CD player.

Chapter **Nine**

Owners' clubs

Like birds of a feather, MX-5, Miata and Roadster owners have a tendency to flock together. There are owners' clubs all over the world, swapping tips and ideas for mods, or addresses for aftermarket suppliers over the internet.

Plenty of owners arrange their holidays to join in with events thousands of miles away on different continents. Some even arrange to borrow one another's cars when they arrive.

Tom Matano signs Clive Southern's boot lid at a meeting of European clubs in Bruges. (Clive Southern)

Events vary from relaxed tours to competitive autocross meetings and concours, but they all offer the opportunity to see some wonderful cars. Plus, on occasion you may bump into one of the car's original designers – the president of the company, Charlie Hughes and his wife are paid up members of the US Miata Owners' Club and are likely to arrive in their own modified Miata.

Tom Matano is another enthusiastic attender of events and is always willing to spend time with owners telling inside stories whether he's in the USA, Europe or Japan. He's also signed a lot of engines with his

'Always Inspired' tag (sometimes countered by Bob Hall's 'Perpetually Perspiring').

The publisher of *Miata Magazine* in the States and a driving force behind the Miata Club, Barbara Beach divides owners into four categories: 'Wine and Cheese', people who like to drive somewhere nice, essentially to socialise; 'Rally and touring types', who enjoy a bit more action from a gymkhana when they arrive. The 'Racers' are autocross fanatics who get very serious about their times. Finally there are the 'Modifiers', who may be looking for performance, or who may just get satisfaction from the engineering that goes into their hot power plant.

Owners in the USA and Canada are probably the most serious when it comes to holding autocross events on shopping mall car parks or airfields, any old piece of tarmac all over the country, and most American club events will include a driving event. In the UK, Europe and down-under in Australia and New Zealand, an exhilarating drive is usually planned as part of the route, and although there may be a driving event when members arrive at their destination the event tends to be smaller and often on grass.

Owners' clubs the world over offer vital services, such as technical advice and preferential insurance schemes. Club events also attract stallholders, offering accessories and showing off their expertise with superbly modified cars.

The exchange of information between clubs has blossomed as more members get on to the net. There is now a flourishing worldwide community of owners and fans on the worldwide web, through Miata.net, the Miata Ring and hundreds of individual club sites. To join in, just get online.

USA and Canada

The US club has always had a privileged position; it was set up as the Miata Club of America even before the car was launched, and US executives have often taken the opportunity to canvas the club for opinions about future product development.

The Californian team working on the original car knew that as soon as their creation escaped into the world, it would have a club. The idea was chewed over by Tom Matano, layout engineer Norman Garrett and his friend since college, Vince Tidwell, who had gone into aviation while Norm headed towards automotive design.

As the Miata's launch approached, Garrett was moving back East to work for Volvo, and he and Vince

US owners enjoy motorsport and those in California also get to keep their hoods down more than most. (*Miata Magazine*)

thought they'd have a go at running the club as an entertaining hobby. As a keen BMW owner, Vince had already been a member of an enthusiasts' club, and to make sure this one was successful, he critiqued a number of existing sports car clubs.

One benefit was that, instead of a newsletter, club members should receive a glossy magazine, sharing the production values of a newstand title. In fact, the excellent *Miata Magazine* is still going strong and you can buy it on the US newstands or a subscription is included with membership – see website www.miataownersclub.com.

Mazda provided the club with a list of proud new owners every month and the response was astonishing. Norman and Vince soon knew that they would not be able to do this alone.

Meanwhile, Barbara Beach and her friend Lyn 'Sky' Vogel had also come up with the idea of starting a club. Barb claims she had originally lost her heart to the RX-7, which she describes as a 'monster with a rotary engine', but a friend had seen some spy shots of a cute little curvy roadster, so very different to American muscle cars or 1970s wedges of cheese and she wanted to be involved. She says: 'When I first saw the Miata, it was smiling at me. I got to take one to an SCCA event in 1989 and everyone was staring and stopping me, because it was so special.'

In fact, it was so special that around 60 people approached Mazda, all suggesting a club, but when Wayne Killen and Rod Bymaster met Barbara, they could see she was clearly someone who could get

Shelby stripes look great in the native land of the Cobra. (*Miata Magazine*)

things done, so they put her in touch with Norman and Vince.

Since then, she has done much to nurture the club and its members and, with her husband, Dr Phil Wolfson, she bought *Miata Magazine* in 1997.

Garrett and Tidwell wanted to bow out of the club, which has since, possibly temporarily, been taken over by Mazda North America and renamed the Miata Owners' Club, but it is still growing and going from strength to strength. The largest event is the massive three-day Miatas at Monterey Festival every year at the Laguna Seca race track in California,

Also, the Miatas have gate-crashed the Concorsa Italiano at Pebble Beach, attending for the last two years as a formal group. So what if the Miata doesn't come from the land of the pasta and the leaning tower? It has more of the spirit and exuberance of Italian sports cars of old than most of the new ones!

There are many chapters all over the States and Canada, all offering the same community support and fun, but driving their Miatas through widely differing and challenging landscapes. Some local clubs drive regularly through deserts, others get to try out the handling on mountain roads. Autocross, or Solo II is the US favourite driving event, but a number of keen

Chocks away! The British meet up at Beaulieu. (Andrew Fearon)

Chocks away! The British meet up at Beaulieu. (Andrew Fearon)

drivers go in for track events. Members of the Wild Rose Chapter in Edmonton, Alberta, however, have also been known to have a go at ice racing.

UK MX-5 Owners' Club

The UK club was a bit of a late-starter compared to the one in the USA. It was originally set up in 1994 by Jane and Paul Grogan, who had previously been members of the US club. When they spotted a fellow UK member in *Miata Magazine*, they thought it was about time the UK had its own club.

So they contacted that member, Tim Robinson, who was somewhat surprised, but just as keen. They sent a mailshot out to UK members of the US club and 28 cars met for the first time on 18 September 1994 at Billing Aquadrome in Northamptonshire.

Mazda's pro-active UK importer, MCL, contacted the club offering support, and remarkably, continued to give support until 1997. Once membership reached 1,000 the original gang felt it was time to step down,

Strict marshalling achieved an aerial view to make Busby Berkeley envious at the British Motor Heritage Centre, Gaydon. (Andrew Fearon)

Sue Duncan has clocked up 107,000 miles in her California (No. 131 of 300). Since Sue was given her cuddly Queen Bee, a swarm have joined her. (Sue Duncan)

decision that had to be taken was whether owners of the numerous Eunos Roadsters, being privately imported into the country should be allowed to join on equal terms with Mazda owners, and the members voted three to one in favour.

UK club members like to meet up for food, drink and a chat, but they love to make the most of the most challenging roads in the UK and Europe on the way. One very popular event is the Isle of Man Tour, taking in the famous TT road course and Jurby race circuit. Members also travel to the Le Mans 24-hour race every year.

Ronald van Kelst from the Belgian club organises tours open to all the European clubs every two years, so the UK club convoyed to Paris in 1998, Bruges in 2000 and the South of France in 2002.

Driving events are usually non-competitive, but people still take their fun seriously. Track days and an annual hillclimb are always popular. Most club events also include a gymkhana, requiring precision driving around cones.

Now the Mk1 MX-5 is accepted as a classic car in the UK, the club also regularly organises stands at larger classic car shows such as the NEC *Classic & Sports Car* Show. This has proved a fruitful ground for gaining new members because so many visitors have wandered up lamenting the fact that their classic roadsters spend more time off the road than on it.

Mazda Motors took over marketing its cars in the UK from MCL in 2001. This means the club's link with Mazda is further away in physical terms, being based in Germany. However, the relationship is actually closer, because the club is now dealing with Mazda direct, rather than with the importer. So for the first time, the club has been invited to Frankfurt and asked for its members' opinions on the hot MPS and the future of the MX-5.

Website: www.mx5oc.co.uk

New Zealand

New Zealand owners generally like to use the car the way Mazda intended, and enjoy the country's wonderful twisty roads. Even though there are relatively few MX-5s and Eunos Roadsters in New Zealand, there are plenty of club events, usually involving a great drive, but occasionally with a hillclimb or track day, so members can really let rip. Local groups also arrange occasional autocross events, but they are usually fairly light-hearted gymkhanas.

Website: www.mx5club.org.nz

so they called for volunteers to create a committee, including current Chairman Allan Legg and his wife Joy.

In mid-2002, the UK club had 4,000 members, including many enthusiastic local groups. One major

The UK Owners' Club tried out the famous TT road racing course on the Isle of Man. (Courtesy Island Photographics, Douglas, Isle of Man)

Members of the New South Wales Owners' Club pose before a driver training day by Ian Luff Motivation Australia. The instructors are John Boston (left) and Ian Kimber in yellow shirts. (Ian Luff)

Fifty MX-5s and their owners from the South Australia Owners' Club attend a wedding at Martindale Hall. (Roger Trethewey)

Roger Trethewey, president of South Australia Owners' Club, puts his right foot down. (Roger Trethewey)

Australia

The vast Australian continent has a single overall owners' club divided into chapters, and these are based in the capital cities of each of the five states. As you can imagine, Australian club activities involve a lot of socialising and barbecues, but also lots of enjoyable driving.

The most popular club driving event is known as a motorkhana. This test of precision driving uses four different circuits, each circuit takes just under a minute and involves reversing and handbrake turns as competitors try to beat the clock.

Some owners enter more serious sporting events, for example in 2002, 12 club members will be entering the New South Wales State Supersprint Championship; seven teams of five members will also compete in the Production Car Racing Association of Australia Championship. (See Chapter Ten)

Website: www.MX5.com.au

Japan

Japan has a large number of local roadster clubs, but no overall umbrella organisation. Two of the largest group are the Roadster Club of Japan (www.open-inc.co.jp/rcoj) and the Kanazawa Roadster Club (www.roadster.hotspace.jp). The latter includes all types of two-seater sports cars including BMW Z3s, Fiat Barchettas and Japanese specials such as the Suzuki Cappucino and Honda Beat, but the majority are Eunos or Mazda Roadsters. This club does not organise any motorsport, but like others, it arranges exhilarating track days.

Japanese owners like to dress up their cars with plenty of accessories and performance parts, and they frequently turn up to events in fancy dress themselves.

Plenty of Roadster drivers do go in for circuit racing, sprints, autocross and hillclimbs, and are serviced by a thriving aftermarket parts industry.

Japanese owners go in for wild body mods. (Andrew Fearon)

A thousand Roadsters, many of which have been modified, are seen parked up around the Hiroshima test track. (Andrew Fearon)

You could ask why he didn't just buy one, but then again perhaps he prefers a car that always starts ... (Andrew Fearon)

Chapter Ten

The MX-5 on track

Club racing was always in the back of the engineers' minds when designing the MX-5, and the car has proved to be just as nimble on the track as they'd hoped. Since its launch, its owners have put the car through adrenaline-pumping events just about every weekend and it has collected an embarrassment of trophies.

However, if you want to race a Mazda, then the USA is the place to be. Owners there can choose between a number of fiercely contested autocross events, time trials, sprints and endurance races. You have to spend money if you want to lift the silverware, though, and most competitors are very serious indeed.

Autocross

Also known as Solo II, Autocross is the US favourite, and most events are sanctioned by the Sports Car Club of America (SCCA Tel. 1-800 770 2055).

This amateur event is cheap to enter, and it is part of the deal that all drivers must help marshal another group.

Competitors drive against the clock around a small road course marked out with cones, usually in a large

Some serious racing Miatas take part in SCCA Autocross events. (Danielle D. Engstrom, SCCA)

US autocrossers set up the cones on any flat piece of concrete they can find. (Danielle D. Engstrom, SCCA)

The Sports Car Club of America oversees a wide variety of racing and autocross events. (*Racer*)

parking lot or on an airfield. The style and length of the course varies considerably by region, but usually contains many linked tight turns, often of increasing or decreasing radii, a few small straight sections and often a slalom section or two. Courses are generally designed to be very tight in order to keep speeds to a safe level.

All sorts of cars compete in appropriate classes, which can include big and powerful machines such as Cadillacs and Lamborghinis, but the compact, agile Miata is perfect. Amateur racers must first participate in two SCCA driving schools before they are eligible to compete in regional races. After six regional events, they can move up to enter national competitions.

The Stock class is popular with Miata owners; cars made from 1994-on are B Stock, those made before are C stock. Despite the stock classification, you are allowed to make some adjustments including the front sway bar, adjustable shocks, a drop-in performance air filter, and you can use DOT-approved race tyres on stock rims.

Miatas have won National Championships in C Stock and B Stock, and their corresponding Ladies' classes for at least the last seven or eight years. In 2000 and 2001, a Miata has won C Street Prepared, in 2001 a Miata also won in the Race-prepared category. Both D Prepared and D Prepared Ladies' events were won by

drivers sharing the same car, which was garage-built by Stan Whitney. This category allows full race preparation, including removing the interior, completely changing the suspension, adding structural stiffness, plus more modifications to the engine than the Street Prepared class allows.

For more details of SCCA Solo classes and regulations, see website www.scca.org/amateur/solo2/index.html and www.wtrscca.org which gives technical and set-up tips.

Road racing

Confusingly for Europeans, this doesn't mean street racing or rallying. In the States, road racing means on a track, and the Miata has also seen plenty of action in endurance races, time trials and production saloon races on race circuits all over the USA.

Miata specialist Flyin' Miata is entering the Open Track Challenge in 2002, which consists of time trials held at different tracks across the USA. Drivers have as many laps as they like to try to achieve their fastest time, but then have to drive off to the next track to do the same again.

The Super Bowl of road racing is the Valvoline Run-offs, named by *Car & Driver* as one of the top 10 racing events in motorsport, where the Miata goes into battle against BMX Z3s, Honda Preludes, and Toyota

Cars in Valvoline Run-offs do occasionally make contact, but Miatas are tough. (Valvoline)

Celicas. The long list of past National Champions reads like a 'who's who' of motor racing, including Bobby Rahal, Jimmy Vassar, Scott Sharp, Skip Barber and Paul Newman. For many winners a National Championship was just a stepping stone on their way to making a name for themselves in motor racing.

Each of the SCCA's eight divisions holds a minimum of six national events where drivers compete for

Most serious American road racers even do without the luxury of a windscreen. (*Racer*)

Valvoline Run-offs are the Super Bowl of road racing, and can be a significant stepping stone for professional racers. (*Racer*)

national points to gain an invitation to the Run-offs. Each contender can participate in as many national races as they want, but can only count the points from their top six finishes.

(For detailed information on the Run-offs, contact the Club Racing Department at SCCA's headquarters in Denver by calling (303) 694-7229 or toll-free at 1-800-770-2055.)

In all, the SCCA has 24 categories for road racing, not all of which would suit a Miata (the sedan class, for example).

The least modified category is the Showroom stock class which is designed for mass-produced cars under seven years old. Small tweaks are allowed, for example, you can change the brake pads, exhaust systems, steering wheel and driver's seat. Roll cages and a harness are compulsory, and steering wheels with airbags should be removed because cars do touch, and an airbag exploding in your face halfway round a corner could be disastrous.

A good place to start is a step up from Showroom stock, in the Improved Touring category. Four- and six-cylinder (and rotary-engined) are split into four categories: A, B, C and S, the Miata sitting in ITA. Engines and transmissions are blueprinted stock

assemblies, but some changes to the suspension are allowed. Most cars in the IT class are five years old or more (the oldest allowed were made in 1968) and it appeals to the budget-conscious racer.

The Production category is one-up from IT, and covers cars including the MG Midget, Lotus Super Seven, Honda Civic and MR2; the Miata is grouped in the fastest category, E Production or EP. Some performance mods are allowed, but the cars must retain their original design, structure and drive layout.

Several cars in the Production classes can be run in more than one class just by changing engines between races, and this allows drivers to enter more than one class at the Run-offs.

Finally there's the very serious Pro Road racing, for Touring Cars in which the engines are built to an exacting spec, with intakes and exhausts tuned for maximum horsepower. The biggest event for these cars is the SCCA Pro Racing Speed World Challenge. See website www.sccapro.com, or www.speedvisionwc.com.

Spec racing

The Spec Miata class is designed to provide an affordable nationwide class in which all regions are using the same rules and regulations. This allows for cross-over region racing and possibly an end of the year Run-off. Most of the races are for an hour or longer.

It was conceived and developed by Import Motorsports and Mazda's competition department in 1999, and approved by the SCCA. NASA (National Auto Sport Association) also officially adopted the class in 2000 and will run Spec Miata in its National series.

Miatas battle it out wheel-to-wheel in the States. Hard-tops add rigidity for racing. (*Racer*)

Clive Southern puts his unique Le Mans limited edition through its paces on a UK club track day. (Clive Southern)

The class includes 1990–93 1.6 and 1994–97 1.8 cars. These cars use Bilstein shock absorbers with adjustable coil-over suspension, Eibach springs and sway bars (front and rear). Steel-braided brake lines, factory stock aluminium rims and Kumbo tyres are also specified.

For more details see website www.Specmiata.com.

UK

Sadly, there is very little MX-5 sports action in the UK. One problem is that MSA regulations for organising events are quite tight.

Autocross events also tend to be shorter, and the courses narrower with tighter turns than in the USA. In these events, or in hillclimbs or track events, the MX-5 goes head-to-head with souped-up, nimble Minis, Vauxhall Novas or Caterhams and Westfields – and it can't compete.

Jonathan McCormack in Belfast still enjoys hillclimbing his 130bhp 1991 Eunos Roadster. He says: 'It's a great little car. I can feel what it's doing and how far I can drift. I scored points in my first year and came fifth once. That's not bad, especially up against specially built cars.'

The UK Owners' Club hopes to get some more motorsport events organised in the near future, but at the moment, the high point for sport in Britain remains the 1991 One-Make Challenge.

1991 One-Make Challenge

MCL organised a one-make challenge for UK enthusiasts for just one year, 1991. The cars were normally aspirated, but tuned to deliver 130bhp, and ran on Koni adjustable shocks and slick tyres, but otherwise they were close to stock. However, safety regulations dictated a fire extinguisher, a racing harness and the world's ugliest roll cage, resembling the poles of an East End market stall.

British Touring Car Championship driver Patrick Watts lifted the cup at the end of the series, having won every race in his Ron Foster-prepared car. He remembers: 'The MX-5 was lots of fun to drive; once we got the suspension set-up sorted, it was very well

Jonathan McCormack's 130bhp hillclimbing Roadster rides Mazdaspeed racing shocks and springs and 15in OZ Racing F1 alloys. (Jonathan McCormack)

mannered. It wasn't very fast down the straight, but it was great on the corners.'

Throughout the season, Watts duelled fiercely with the young Mark Lemmer who also went on to have a successful career in BTCC. Watts says: 'The cars were so close in power, it was very hard to keep the next guy behind you. Everyone came together on the corners and it was a real battle, a lot of cars crashed.'

The championship only saw one season because it failed to attract adequate sponsorship. The decision not to continue in 1992 may also have been influenced by a serious accident at Silverstone in which well-

The British One-Marque Championship showcased some fast and furious driving in 1991. (LAT)

known sports photographer Gary Hawkins lost a leg.

Some of the cars continued to be used for sprints, while others were converted back to road cars.

Patrick Watts went on to drive for Peugeot and Mazda in the British Touring Car Championships and won the Australian Touring Car Championship before retiring.

The pack snakes around the chicane at Monza September 2001, racing nose-to-bumper in the Mazda Sport Cup 2000. (Astra Racing)

Massimiliano Mugelli proves you don't need all four wheels to get an MX-5 round a corner. (Astra Racing)

Europe

The Mazda Sport Cup is an annual European racing series, giving keen MX-5 racers the chance to drive on such famous circuits as Monza and Imola. It visits nine circuits in all, between April and October. The cars are prepared by Astra Racing near Turin in Italy, known worldwide for preparing racing cars and for manufacturing prototypes and high-performance components.

The cars use the standard normally aspirated 1,839cc engine with a compression ratio of 9.5:1, stoked up to deliver 168bhp. The suspension is tightened up using Fly Competition dampers and the anchors are provided by brake discs of 250mm in diameter, ventilated at the

Elisa Giordan 'la Pantera Rosa' (Pink Panther) puts her foot down at the A1 Ring. (Astra Racing)

front. The cars run on 6.5in x 15 Speedline wheels with Avon performance tyres.

The popular series is supported by Mazda Motor Italia Spa, and it gives away plenty of silverware for classes including Winner, Ladies, Under 25s and Over 40s.

No British drivers have entered so far, but it is said that when it started, lots of discarded hoods were snapped up by the UK club. For more details, see website www.astraracing.com.

Australia

Australian MX-5 enthusiasts can enter a number of different racing formulas overseen by the Confederation of Australian Motor Sport (CAMS) including Production Sports Car racing and Supersprints. The latter is a form of circuit time trials, in which cars from stock to fully developed racing cars compete in different classes in races of between five and 12 laps.

In 2002, 12 MX-5s will compete in the New South Wales State Supersprint Championship to be conducted over eight rounds at three different circuits. Over the past three years, the MX-5 Club has won the Club Championship twice, coming third on the other.

Seven teams of five cars will also compete in the Production Sports Car Racing Association of Australia Championship, battling Toyota MR2s and MGFs in the Class C category.

Fast and furious action at Oran Park, Sydney; Anthony Robson leads a motley crew. (dh-photo.com)

The craziest event of the year is the National 1,000km event for V8 supercars at the Mount Panorama track west of Sydney, at Bathurst.

Clubs also organise Regularities, where a driver nominates their expected lap time and endeavours to complete eight laps of the circuit keeping as close to that lap time as possible.

Mike Hicks of the Mazda MX-5 Club of New South Wales says that a large number of cars involved in

Brad Douglass goes for it at the Eastern Creek circuit near Sydney. (dh-photo.com)

MX-5s down-under mix it with everything from Cobras and Morgans to Porsches and the odd Lotus Elise in the Production Sports Cars class. (dh-photo.com)

racing are early-model Roadsters imported cheaply from Japan, which cannot be registered for the road as they do not conform to Australia's Design Rules.

Trim, carpets, etc are stripped out to reduce weight and a solid roll-bar fitted. Most competitors will invest in competition springs, shocks, brakes, anti-roll bars, and a limited-slip differential and wider wheels, and the standard engines will be tweaked and tuned for more power.

The NSW club also holds club practice days for up to 40 cars at a time as an introduction to motorsport.

New Zealand

Although members are keen drivers, not many MX-5s were imported to New Zealand, so although individual members may enter production saloon races, motorsport tends to be limited to local motorkhanas and hillclimbs.

Racing Roadsters line up ready for action in Japan. (Andrew Fearon)

Mods and accessories

The MX-5 might be a volume seller, but you never see two the same. The urge to add just a little personal touch is irresistible and the scope for making your car individual is enormous.

You can smarten it up by retrimming the seats and adding bright touches to the interior, you can add a body kit, choose from a vast mass of accessories, or stoke up the engine.

The engineers had their way when they were building it, so this is a tough little car and its chassis and structure can handle a phenomenal amount of power. Now the older models are getting cheaper and younger buyers can afford them, the number of seriously hot cars is rising. Keith Tanner from US performance specialist Flyin' Miata says: 'The great thing is that it's so reliable, you can afford to spend the money on mods, rather than just keeping it healthy.'

What owners do to their cars can depend on where they live. In America, boosting power is popular, but in Switzerland, regulations forbid any serious engine work, so enthusiasts go for wild body kits. In Germany, too, TUV regulations forbid a change of brakes or ECU, so again, the conversions tend to be for show rather than go. The Japanese love to dress up their cars, too, so most of the wildest body kits and brightest chrome goodies come from Germany or Japan.

The UK Owners' Club now has sections of its concours competition for Hot 5, for those with performance to match the description, or Cool 5 for those that just look fabulous.

The best place to look for inspiration or parts is on the net. A number of club and enthusiasts' sites offer reviews of parts people have bought with praise or complaints about their user-friendliness. Miata.net has reviews of products, and a chart showing which parts from the MX-5 Mk1 and Mk2/3 are interchangeable. Or

www.mx5.mods.co.uk has a running top 10 most popular mods (usually headed by the good old K&N filter). This site also provides a forum for modifiers to show off their engineering triumphs, or warn of their disasters. If you register here, the team will also answer your queries on line.

Just for fun, Keith Tanner's site lets you try different stripes or wheels on your car to see how they look, but be warned, he doesn't sell either, and the products shown may not be up to date. (Look for his site on Miata.net.)

Cabin

The MX-5's cockpit is neat and orderly, but it doesn't live up to the promise of the gorgeous curvy exterior. It says a lot that one of the most popular MX-5/Miata mods is a pair of chrome air vent rings.

Another favourite is a set of white dials, as fitted to the production Mk3. You can actually have them in most colours, or go for a fluorescent look. The walnut dashboards of the 1960s may have been outlawed by safety legislation (and the realisation that you don't want to headbutt a plank in the case of an accident), but there are plenty of other options now. Companies such as Autotech Designs and Moss can sell you dash and console veneer inserts in burr walnut, carbon fibre, brushed aluminium or pearl-effect.

There are also plenty of companies offering wood steering wheels, gear levers and handbrake handles. Think hard before interfering with a steering wheel fitted with an airbag, however. It may not look stylish, but your safety is more important, and you might find your car is harder to sell on.

Alloy gear levers are more fashionable in new cars at the moment, following the example of racing cars and the Ford Puma. Perhaps the most extreme option,

Above: Charlotte Nadin transformed the interior of her Mk2 California into what she believes it should have been. (Dougie Firth)

Below: Some go even further. This Japanese owner didn't understand the phrase 'over the top'. (Andrew Fearon)

though, comes from KG Works, which produces a Ferrari-style metal open gate.

Touring

It's great to let the MX-5 really stretch its legs over twisting mountains roads, the difficulty comes if you don't have a butler to drive ahead with the luggage.

However, a number of companies, such as Jaz bags, have come to the aid of the determined tourer.

One option is a bag to fit behind the seats, although sticking up slightly from the rear deck. You can opt for a complete set of bags which fit together like a three-dimensional jigsaw to use up every inch of boot space. Or, if you have a Mk1, which carries its spare wheel in the boot, there are circular bags tailored to fit into the centre of the spare.

Of course, another option is the good old rear boot rack, and there are a number to choose from which do not require any drilling into the lid.

Most owners get fed up quite quickly with the romantic idea of wind in the hair, or rather down the back of the neck, so fitting a windstop is probably a good idea before you set off. Again, there are a number on the market, but most people's favourite is the Oris Windstop. Although quite expensive, it virtually eliminates wind buffeting, and is reckoned to be better

Oris Windstop is reckoned to be better than the standard item in the Mk2 and Mk3. (Moss Europe)

than the standard item provided on the Mk2 or Mk3. It fits easily with two screws, and can be left in place when you put the hood up. Serious Automotive also offers an Oris Windstop incorporated into a Hard Dog roll-over bar.

A luggage rack that can be fitted without drilling is the best option. (Moss Europe)

Maztek's Richard Ducommun found an old-stock Finish Line body kit intended for the Le Mans; his Mk1 is lowered and uses Tokico adjustable springs and dampers. (Dougie Firth)

A Jackson Racing supercharger with a Pacecharge cooler boosts Richard's 1.6-litre engine to 200bhp. (Dougie Firth)

Dressing up

One of the most popular body decorations in the States is a set of front-to-rear white stripes, echoing Carroll Shelby's colours for the famous Cobra. You can buy stripes from most graphics suppliers, or try specialists, The Mroad.

Just for fun, you can try out different coloured stripes on Keith Tanner's site: Keith@miata.net/stripes.

Body kits may add aerodynamic effects, or simply give a more individual look. Some of these pick up on ideas show-cased by MX-5 concept cars, for example, twin-headlamps peering from beneath half-closed

This impressive European Dodge Viper lookalike was spotted in Bruges by Clive Southern. (Clive Southern)

The European Mk1 has M Speedster-style twin headlamps and Shelby stripes. (Clive Southern)

A whale-tail boot spoiler is fitted to Allan Legg's Mk2 Anniversary. (James Mann)

Modified cars spotted by Andrew Fearon in the USA; one has an M Speedster-style aerodeck. (Andrew Fearon)

pop-ups echo the muscular M Speedster of 1995. This converson is offered by BrainStorm, Donutz and Moss.

Some owners pay homage to other more expensive sports cars. For example, MX-5s have been spotted in Europe giving good impressions of a Dodge Viper, a miniature Ferrari, or even a Lotus Elan.

Sporty whale-tail boot spoilers are another popular option. For outrageous body kits, have a look on the web at Eribuni Corporation, and KG Works.

Roll-over bars are also fitted for either safety or style. In fact, because of litigation concerns in the States, these are often referred to as style bars.

A number of companies offer single or double hoops bolted behind the seats. If you're racing, however, you may need a heavier-duty roll cage, such as those produced by Hard Dog Fabrication.

Soft-tops

Hoods will generally last eight to 10 years, although sadly, the binding around the edges tends to dry out and crack long before the hood fabric wears out. When the time comes to replace it, you could splash out on an attractive high-quality hood in duck or canvas. Or

you can buy a new replacement because the Mk2 and Mk3 hood can be made to fit an earlier car.

The Mk1 and Mk2/3 hoods are similar apart from their rear windows. On the Mk1, the plastic window has to be zipped out and laid flat before the hood is folded to prevent creasing and damage. The hood fabric is fixed to the hoops, and is pulled back with it.

As you push the Mk2 hood back, the fabric slides over the hoops and the glass window is lowered to lie flat behind the rear seats. So the Mk2 hood and window can be made to fit the Mk1 frame with a relatively simple alteration to allow it to slide over the hoops. Matt Clark of Matt Developments sells a 'zip by-pass kit' to allow this. See www.Miata.net/garage for detailed instructions.

Matt can also offer a glass window conversion for a Mk1 hood using 2CV rear glass. This can be sewn-in Mk2 style, or you can have a zip. This allows you to zip out the window and lay it down just like the original plastic version, to get some fresh air while keeping the

This Mk1 Limited Edition has a high-quality aftermarket duck hood with a heated glass window. (James Mann)

Matt Developments can fit a glass rear window to a Mk1 hood. (Matt Clark)

hood up (as many standard Mk1 owners like to do). This has proved so popular, Moss has also developed a zip-out glass window.

Another interesting option from Matt Developments is an easy-lift system kit for the hood, featuring small gas struts. These allow even small owners to raise or lower the hood from inside the car – for example at traffic lights – should there be a cloudburst.

If you're in the UK, you can call London-based Matt Clark (Tel. 020 8803 1122) or see his website: www.mattdevelopments.co.uk. His products are also stocked by BrainStorm.

Hard-tops

Hard-tops for the Mazda and Eunos Roadster and the Mk1 and Mk2 are interchangeable, but their rubber seals are different. So they will fit without any modification, but will probably leak unless you change the seal.

Hard-tops are only available from dealers in the colours current at the time, so you will probably have to fork out for a respray whether you buy new or second-hand.

Moss can also offer a budget glassfibre hood if you really want to keep the weather out, but don't want to stump up for a full factory version. This is, of course, lighter than the factory original, which is a plus for economy and performance, but it won't keep the body as rigid as a metal top.

PERFORMANCE MODIFICATIONS AND TUNING

Owners have been hotting up their MX-5s since it first roared out of the factory and, as prices fall and younger people are getting behind the wheel, the conversions are becoming wilder, both in looks and extra power.

The MX-5 can handle plenty of power; it won't fall apart, and it will still handle tidily even with a V8 under the bonnet. That said, every mod will affect the way the car drives. So it's best to sit down and come up with an overall plan before starting to add performance parts on an ad hoc basis.

Obviously, if you hot up the engine, you'll have to look at your suspension and your brakes, or you won't be able to exploit the power.

However, one way to gain more power instantly is to rev the car far higher than most owners ever do. The redline is way up at 7,000rpm, and letting the needle hit it won't damage a well maintained engine, even if it will be letting out quite a roar. Try it before reading on.

Engine tuning

Mazda's engineering team will probably have beaten you to most of the traditional methods of squeezing a few more horsepower out of an engine. Both the 1.6 and 1.8 are extremely efficient 16-valve units each benefiting from excellent ignition and fuel injection systems and a highly tuned intake manifold. The team also had some pointers from the proven 323 GTX turbo, so just like its boosted cousin, the MX-5's engine was given lighter rotating components, a windage tray for the sump and a high compression ratio. Nevertheless, there are areas in which you can cut into the margins left by the original engineers to make sure the car is smooth and economical for everyday use.

The MX-5's weakest point is its low-rev pull, so the cheapest way to tweak a little more power out of your car is to increase the basic ignition timing from the stock 10 BTDC (before top dead centre) to 18 BTDC. This should give around 20 per cent more torque at 1,000rpm, but you will have to stick to petrol of 92 octane or greater to avoid detonation or 'knock'. If you regularly rev to 6,500rpm or more, then 14 will suit your driving style better. It will give you around two more horsepower and move the power band up by around 400rpm.

More juice?

A traditional way to boost power is to pump in more fuel, but if anything the Mazda runs a little too rich, and you won't have enough air in the chamber to burn the extra fuel unless you opt for forced induction (either supercharging or turbocharging). Then you can either fit a high-performance fuel pump, increase fuel rail pressure or go for the more expensive option of fitting larger injectors.

Let it breathe

The most effective way to hot up your engine is to help it breathe more easily, although how far you go depends on how much power you want, and how much you are willing to spend. The aim is to allow your Mazda to suck in more clean, cool air to help the fuel burn efficiently, creating a nice big bang in the combustion chamber and then to expel the burnt gases as quickly as possible.

In fact, the best way to start is back to front, because there's no point in your engine gulping in air, if it is then trying to push the burnt gases out through a restrictive stock system. You'll just end up with an asthmatic Five.

The same principles apply as you replace sections of the exhaust system. If you don't want to splash out on an entire system all at once, then start by replacing the rear box (or muffler in Yankee-speak) first, then slot in a performance cat, and if you still want more power, invest in a performance exhaust manifold (header).

Replacement rear sections often include a 'cat-back' system which has a larger-diameter pipe leading from the catalytic converter. It's well worth considering a high-flow cat if your car has done 50,000 miles or more, because the original will be giving up the ghost soon anyway.

Plenty of power figures are bandied around by the various parts manufacturers, but replacing your entire exhaust system can boost your output by close to 20 per cent. A simple item such as a cat-back muffler alone can add 7bhp and 5lb ft of torque.

There are a large number of stainless steel systems promising maximum air flow on the market, but it is best to invest in a well-known name such as Jackson Racing, Moss or Borla. Cheaper systems can set up an annoying resonance or boom which can ruin the driving experience. You should also look for a system with a minimum of twists and bends or welds because these will simply add resistance.

Breathing in

Aftermarket parts to help your MX-5 inhale range from a simple, less-restrictive air filter to turbochargers and superchargers. The popular K&N filter gives the engine a slightly more growly note as well as boosting power and improving throttle response. The Jackson Racing dual-stage air filter is made of pre-oiled foam. It promises an extra 3bhp and you can buy a cleaning kit to keep it effective.

A number of suppliers also offer a tuned induction unit to replace the stock air-filter box, which gives the air a smoother journey.

These changes may simply shift the available power up the rev range, but mid-range power is what you need if you want to overtake that caravan and get a free stretch of road.

The next step up is to fit a cold-air induction kit. This

A free-flow stainless steel exhaust system allows your MX-5 to breathe more easily; it's best to start replacing the system from the back. (Moss Europe)

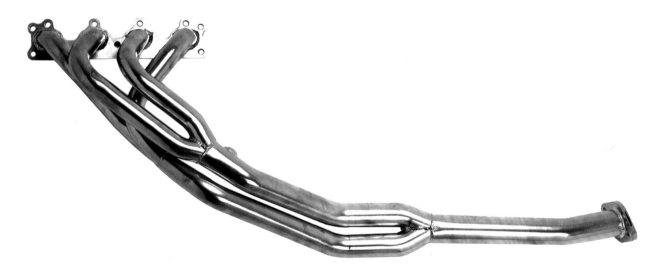

replaces the stock intake tract up to the throttle body. It incorporates a high-performance air filter, and works by directing cold air from ahead of the radiator into a tuned airbox. It passes through an airflow meter to let the engine's ECU know what's going on and then into the throttle body with increased velocity. These kits are offered by Jackson Racing, BrainStorm, Racing Beat and the Japanese tuner HKS. They can gain a significant boost of 12–14bhp for a very reasonable price.

If this doesn't quench your thirst for power, then the next step is forced induction – bolting on a turbo or a supercharger.

Supercharging versus Turbocharging

The debate about which method of getting that surge is best has been raging since 1989. Rod Millen and BBR went for the turbo option, but when layout engineer Norman Garrett left Mazda in 1989, he approached Eaton Superchargers to create a small unit specially for the Miata. This is still around, now known as the Jackson Racing Sebring supercharger and is sold by Moss among many others.

Both methods work by forcing more fresh air into the cylinders to burn more fuel and so create more power. Turbos are driven by exhaust gases from the engine and are usually used in conjunction with an intercooler, which chills the air before it goes into the engine to boost power even further. Superchargers are powered directly from the engine via a belt. Jackson Racing has produced upgrades for its supercharger to

set it spinning even faster, so increasing boost by up to 20 per cent.

Superchargers, or blowers, deliver more low-down grunt, so their enthusiasts claim they are better for everyday use. With a turbo, the extra oomph kicks in higher up the rev range, and there can be a delay between your right foot pressing the pedal and a fierce kick in the back – the dreaded turbo lag – but the turbo keeps on pushing long after the supercharger has run out of breath. In fact, even the BBR and Le Mans turbos deliver their power very smoothly, with no obvious lag, and modern turbos are improving all the time.

A water injection system can be used with either the turbo or the blower. This sprays water through a fine nozzle into the intake charge where it atomises and soaks up the heat created by either system.

If it is not controlled, this heat can cause damaging detonation. Another method of controlling this is simply to retard the timing, but the result can be a sluggish, low rpm response. Using water injection to cool the air down allows more ignition advance, and so better throttle response.

Today, opinion is swinging strongly in the direction of the sophisticated 21st century turbo over the 'blower'. Both Keith Tanner of Flyin' Miata in the States and Richard Ducommun of Maztek in the UK reported independently that a large number of owners were actually coming in to have their superchargers stripped out and replaced by turbos.

One reason, Keith suggests, is that the Sebring supercharger is not ideal for later models, and far more

The BBR Turbo engine in Doug Nadin's Le Mans is very original. (Dougie Firth)

The same engine in Clive Southern's Le Mans has been transformed into a work of art. (Dougie Firth)

development work has been done on the various turbo systems. He says: 'The main advances being made now are in the electronics rather than the turbos themselves, which are well understood technology; we don't just rechip, we put in a full replacement ECU.'

A second factor is that, as the prices of used MX-5s go down, younger owners are demanding the increased top-end power delivered by a turbo.

He says: 'Older drivers usually want the car driveable and easy to live with. The kids are interested in quarter-mile times, and they're not as bothered about the handling.'

It's interesting to note that both Rod Millen and Brodie Brittain Racing have now given up offering performance parts for the MX-5/Miata due, they say to reduced demand, while Flyin' Miata, which is always working to find more extreme power, is clearly becoming one of the market leaders in this area.

The company is currently preparing a racing Miata using a 1995 block from Mazda's cousin, Kia, bored out and fitted with new pistons, rods and crank. This car currently puts out 340hp at the wheels thanks to 22lb of boost, and Keith reckons there is more to come.

Turbocharging is also a popular option in New Zealand, because the Mazda 323 GTX 4WD Turbo models are frequently imported, and it is reasonably straightforward to strip out the turbo and fit it to the MX-5, although a new manifold and a few other mods are required.

A trip to the machine shop

One way to optimise your engine's breathing is to make sure the intake and exhaust manifold ports mate precisely with those of the cylinder head. Slight variations in the casting process may mean that the head ports will not quite match, but you can have them both removed and machined. To check for a mismatch, remove the manifold, make a 'gasket' in cardboard and then hold it up to the cylinder head.

While you're at it, the cylinder head can be 'ported' to make the transition between the combustion chamber and the ports as smooth as possible.

Take a look at the valve seats, too. These should not be too narrow, an intake landing should be no less than 0.060in wide, an exhaust valve seat should be 0.075in wide. It is best to ask for triple-cut valve and seat details, because the airflow from port wall to valve seat and into the combustion chamber will be smoother than rushing over a 45° angle.

If you want to increase the compression ratio, you

This Eunos Roadster in Australia has been boosted by the turbo from the Mazda's Familia 1.8 engine. (Roger Trethewey)

can have the cylinder head milled. The minimum cylinder-head height quoted by Mazda is 133.8mm, which is as low as you can go for some racing classes. It is possible to take it lower, though, because the cambelt has a tensioner which can take up the slack of a lower cam-pulley-to-crankshaft dimension.

Every 0.065in you mill off the head removes about 0.15cu in (2.5cc) from the chamber and increases compression approximately half a compression-ratio point.

If you're going for a forced-induction engine it's best just to have the head smoothed over with a very light milling, because you'll need the greater volume in the combustion chamber.

Camshaft

You can buy aftermarket high-lift cams from companies such as the Japanese performance specialists. The improvements will not be dramatic, but if you are going for ultimate power, they will shift the power peak a little higher up the range. Racers should also consider having the cam-bearing bores align-honed or align-bored.

Crankshaft

The life of your hard-working crankshaft can be extended by nitriding. Micropolishing with ultra-fine emery paper will reduce surface friction with bearings.

For smoother running, you should also get the con rods balanced and cleaned up. They should all weigh the same, and all rough casting marks should be removed. Shot peening will create a stronger, harder surface.

If you are fitting a turbo or supercharger, you should consider a set of heavy-duty rods, for example, those from the 323 GTX are stronger than those of the stock MX-5, but they are heavier.

Flywheel

A lighter flywheel allows the engine to spin more quickly because of its reduced rotational inertia. The engine revs will drop faster between gearshifts, too.

The stock item weighs 18lb (8kg), but you can buy much lighter replacements, including aluminium versions weighing just 4lb (1.8kg). Try performance suppliers such as BrainStorm and Racing Beat.

A 5.0-litre Mustang V8 fits nicely in the Miata engine bay and the chassis can handle it. (Andew Fearon)

More cubic inches

Both the 1.6 and 1.8 engines have enough metal in them to allow you to overbore the cylinder and gain more capacity. You can bore out the 1.6 by 0.040in to give 24.992cu in (409.6cc) per cylinder, 2.549cu in (41.8cc) more than the stock engine, which is worth about 3 horsepower. The new compression ratio will be up to 9.6:1.

On the 1.8, the 0.040in overbore will give you an added 2.770cu in (45.4cc) and about 3.3 more horsepower and a compression ratio of 9.2:1.

For the 1.6 owner, a more effective way to gain more capacity is to shoehorn in a 1.8-litre engine. The swap is pretty simple and the transmissions are the same. However, adapting the wiring is a pig of a job.

The two exhaust systems and manifolds are quite different, but if you are going as far as swapping an engine, you'll probably be changing the exhaust anyway.

Creating a Monster

There's something irresistibly seductive about the rumble of a V8. So whatever the car, someone will always try to lever one in – after all, it worked for Carroll Shelby and Ken Miles, when they squeezed a V8 into a Sunbeam Alpine to create the Tiger.

Remarkably, the equation of V8 into Mazda will go. David Hops of Monster Motorsports eased a 5.0-litre Mustang V8 into a Miata's engine bay shortly after the car arrived in the USA, creating the first Monster Miata.

It sounds like a recipe for terminal understeer, but the 302cu in (4,949.8cc) Ford V8 fits relatively easily beneath the Mazda's bonnet and weighs only 250lb (113kg) more than the four-cylinder unit it replaces. With sufficient reinforcements to the body, the Monster remains a balanced and nimble sports car.

A standard 302 Monster can sprint to 60mph (96kph) in 4.8 seconds and to a quarter-mile in 12.6 seconds, recording 111.6mph (179.6kph) as it passes the marker. However David Hops went on to pushing the envelope even further with the Mega-Monster, adding a Kenne Bell supercharger to boost power to 400bhp and torque to 375lb ft. A Ford Thunderbird limited-slip differential and a number of frame reinforcements helped the car deal with the extra power. The five-bolt hubs, rotors and calipers from the third generation RX-7 R1 made sure it stopped again.

The Mega-Monster was capable of 0–60mph in 4.2 seconds, or the quarter-mile in 12.6 seconds at 111.6mph. This beat a Dodge Viper (0–60mph 4.5sec, standing quarter 13.2/112.1) or a Corvette ZR1 (0–60mph 5.2sec, standing quarter 13.6/106).

If this sounds like the car for you, contact Monster Motorsports in Escondido California (Tel. 619 738 7592) or Panache in San Marcos (Tel. 760 510 9682).

Other V8 fans have followed the Monster lead, in Britain, the more compact ex-Buick Rover V8 is plentiful and cheap. An English contributor to www.MX5mods.co.uk, calling himself simply 'Bob', has fitted one in his Eunos Roadster, and reckons his 220bhp 3.5-litre car is 'a pussycat' to drive, compared with a TVR.

The New Zealand owners' club recently held an entire meeting of V8 Mazdas using either Holden V8s, or the 4.0-litre Lexus LC400 (Toyota Soarer) engine.

In Australia, regulations forbid a straight transplant, however Bullet Cars, now owned by AEC, offers an extreme alternative. To create its Bullet Roadster, the company imports MX-5 bodyshells from Japan, stretches the wheelbase by 70mm and constructs its own box-section chassis. It then fits the all-alloy quad-cam 4.0-litre Lexus V8. For the muscular SS, it then bolts on a supercharger. The prototypes for both have undergone rigorous homologation tests and the Bullet V8s are sold as new cars.

With a 429bhp and 405lb ft, the pounding SS could give a Porsche 911 Turbo a fright. However, thanks to a 53/47 per cent weight distribution and the slightly longer wheelbase, it retains much of the MX-5's supreme balance (it has some serious Brembo brakes, too). You can snap up a normally aspirated Bullet Roadster for $98,000 or the SS for $118,000.

Nitrous injection

If you really want your MX-5 to fly, then you can join the growing number of drivers who have turned to the drag racer's favourite tipple: nitrous oxide.

As mentioned above, the key to getting more power from your engine is to burn more fuel, and this is usually accomplished by adding air.

Nitrous contains more oxygen than normal air, so you effectively feed your car 'super air'.

At the high temperatures inside the cylinders of your engine, the nitrous oxide molecule breaks open, releasing its oxygen atom. This oxygen allows more fuel to be burned, creating higher cylinder pressures, and more power.

The left-over nitrogen acts as a buffer to keep the reaction under control, and is then ejected with the rest of the exhaust gases.

A separate, very useful feature of nitrous is its cooling effect. When liquid nitrous at the nozzle is released into the intake stream, it instantly turns into a gas. The boiling temperature of nitrous oxide is –127°F. This has a serious cooling effect on the entire intake charge. Since an 11°F drop in charge temperature correlates with roughly one per cent gain in power, this cooling effect alone can produce a 5–8 per cent gain in power.

For more information about how to fit a nitrous kit, with pictures of gased-up cars in action, go to www.n2omx5.com or www.mongrelms.homestead.com/mx5nitrous.

Body building
Chassis rigidity
Mazda stiffened up the chassis in 1992 and more seriously in 1994, mainly to reduce vibration. Earlier cars can easily be fitted with braces for the front and rear subframes, plus cockpit braces which run between the shoulder harness mounting points.

Another popular option to stiffen up the rear bulkhead is to fit a roll-over bar (in the litigious USA these must be known as 'style bars') which can usually be fitted to the seatbelt turrets.

For ultimate stiffness, you can opt for a full roll cage, and there are a number on the market, including the well-known Hard Dog item. However in the UK, the height of the cage required for sport makes the soft-top difficult to fit with one in place.

Wheels

If you're worried about preserving your car's supremely balanced handling, then think hard before changing your car's wheels. Enough space was provided inside the wheel arch to use snowchains, so it is possible to fit up to an 18in wheel with low-profile rubber. This will look handsome, but you'll ruin the finely tuned handling of your Mazda.

The Mk1's original alloys are some of the lightest ever fitted to a mass-production car and they were fitted with special lightweight Dunlops. Both were commissioned to reduce unsprung weight, so even the alloy wheels fitted to special editions by local distributors such as MCL in the UK, can spoil the optimum balance created in Hiroshima.

So, if you are going to change the wheels, go for the lightest possible option.

The 1994 five-spoke wheels weigh just 10.3lb (4.7kg), or even less if polished, and are highly prized, but unfortunately rare.

The BBS 15in wheel, created using a high-pressure forging process weighs just 9.6lb (4.4kg), or the polished M-edition wheel is also a good choice if you can find one. (Polishing reduces weight even further.)

The Mk2 MX-5 has 15in tyre and wheel combinations available from the factory which can be retrofitted to Mk1s.

Wire wheels tend to be heavy and so are best avoided. (They're a menace to clean, too.)

The rolling diameter of the stock Miata wheel and tyre combination is 22.7in. The bigger the wheel, the lower the profile of the tyre must be. If you go higher than 23.2in, it will affect your speed readings and your gear ratios.

The taller the rolling height, the taller the overall gear ratio will be and the less brisk your acceleration will be.

The collar which keeps the wheel centred is 54mm in diameter. So it is essential that the hubcentric collar diameter of an aftermarket wheel matches this.

The original wheels have a 45mm offset to make room for the brake calipers and to fit into Mazda's family wheel system, however this is not a standard size. Most aftermarket wheels have an offset of 35–37mm. This will fit the car and look pretty smart, but will create some unacceptable handling quirks and

lead to premature wear of your suspension bushes. Just listen for the rattles and crashes over potholes.

A good compromise is the Panasport 14 or 15-inch eight-spoke Minilite-lookalike which is light, has a 45mm offset and an attractive polished aluminium finish. (Available from Moss.)

Tyres

You can sharpen up the MX-5's handling even more with a set of performance tyres. The US Miata Owners' Club favourites in the inexpensive bracket are the Dunlop D60 and Yokohama A509.

Or you can upgrade to a premium tyre such as the Dunlop SP-8000 or Michelin Pilot 4. These will provide even greater grip and performance.

Remember that fitting a wider tyre doesn't necessarily mean more grip if it is not staying flat on the tarmac; it may just change the shape of the contact patch rather than putting more rubber on the ground. So if you're going this route, you also need to alter the suspension.

Remember, too, that a larger tyre weighs more and takes longer to get warm. The widest tyre a MX-5 can wear is 195mm of tread width.

Suspension

Ride comfort and superb handling are natural enemies, one requiring a softer set-up, the other needing a firm platform, and well controlled body roll.

It is a compromise engineers have to struggle with, keeping a close eye on their customers. National tastes are quite different, too. Americans drive on long straight roads for hours at a time, and so Europeans find the typical yank's ride too wallowy. US drivers find European suspension set-ups, designed for wriggly roads strewn with hairpins, very hard on the backside.

Mazda's engineers achieved something quite extraordinary with the MX-5. The ride is firm, but far from uncomfortable, and its body control is supreme as it rails around the tightest bends.

Its suspension is already too good to need the extra roll bars (or sway bars) frequently fitted to cars to sharpen up their handling. If the engine's power has been boosted, some extra tweaks may be required to keep the new set-up under control, or owners may choose to sacrifice a little comfort for even sharper handling.

Fitting shorter, stiffer springs and performance shocks will firm up the suspension to give flatter cornering. If you are racing regularly, a number of

companies offer short springs for the MX-5, which will lower the car by up to 2in, however, if you drop it by more than an inch, you'll have to raise the steering rack to avoid 'bump steer'. Go down another 0.25in and you will have to trim the rubber bump stops, too.

If your springs are too stiff, you will actually lose traction as the wheels need enough travel to clamber over bumps – wheels in the air don't grip or steer. The best way to lower your MX-5 is by fitting adjustable shock absorbers, such as the popular Koni. In fact, after a set of performance tyres, the next best way to improve ride and handling quality is to fit performance shock absorbers.

The Konis are adjustable for damping and allow you to lower the ride height of your car in seconds while still using the stock springs. An added benefit is that when it starts to wear, a turn of the knob will dial back in any lost damping force.

A number of shocks, including those by Carrera also have an adjustable lower cap or spring perch which can be moved up and down to easily change the ride height.

You can also buy threaded sleeves to create a finely adjustable lower spring perch.

Legal LSD

A limited-slip differential prevents one wheel from spinning uselessly under power, while the matching wheel is stationary. It helps the car grip in extreme conditions such as an icy road or a sharp corner on a race track.

The first to be offered for the MX-5 was a simple viscous limited-slip diff made up of a set of plates

Panasport Minilite-lookalike wheels are comparatively light, and so should not upset your handling like other aftermarket alloys. (Moss Europe)

connected to each axle, running in a bath of silicone fluid. The plates don't touch, but as one spins faster than the other, the silicone firms up under the shearing force and resists the differing speeds.

This was an option, but can be retrofitted without too much of a problem.

From 1994, the Torsen gear differential was introduced, and this long-lasting and tough unit provides excellent traction.

Again, it is relatively simple to retrofit. However, if you are fitting a Torsen differential from a 1996 or later car into a 1994 or 1995 car, you'll need to use the later-style halfshafts introduced that year. That will mean swapping the diff, halfshafts and driveshaft.

From 1997, Mazda introduced the Torsen Type 2, which was cheaper to manufacture (and sell) than the Type 1 and has a higher-bias ratio, so this is a better option. The part number is MM02-27-200A.

Transmission

The MX-5's gearbox is quite simply one of the best on the market. Its quick-shifting action is a delight, and it is strong, so it is best left just as it is. However, you might consider a stronger clutch if you are going for a radical power hike.

A number of gear sets are offered by the aftermarket manufacturers to allow you to change up a little later, but changing the final drive is probably best left to serious racers.

Chapter **Twelve**

Keeping your car healthy

Protecting the body

An accessory front grille not only looks smart, but it also protects the vulnerable radiator. Stones thrown up from the road have been known to go right through the aluminium rad, landing owners with a large bill.

An accessory grille will protect the aluminium radiator from stones. Tie-down hooks inside the 'mouth' must not be used as tow hooks. (James Mann)

Note, too, that the 'eyes' inside the front 'mouth' are tie-down hooks to secure the car on a trailer; they must not be used to tow the car.

The Mk1's boot has its battery on the right-hand side, but on the inside the thin metal of the wing has nothing to protect it from golf clubs and the like sliding into it as the car takes a corner. Some cars actually have small dents on the wing. You can now buy a little black pad from accessories companies to protect it.

Early cars are beginning to show signs of rust in the

The Atlantic design fender bag will protect the rear wing from shifting luggage or golf clubs when cornering. (Moss Europe)

The Atlantic design fender bag will protect the rear wing from shifting luggage or golf clubs when cornering. (Moss Europe)

sills and chassis rails, so if you want to protect your car, buy a Waxoyl kit and pump in plenty of the black (or brown) stuff now!

UK club members have been impressed with Wonder Wax by CarPlan, for polishing and protecting paintwork. Be aware that paint on early cars is quite thin, and if you polish it too much you can go right through to the primer.

Alloy wheels were frequently only laquered on one side, and so consider taking them off, and cleaning them up to inspect their condition. It may be worth having them sandblasted and laquered to protect them in the future. It's a very good idea to have a set of plain steel wheels to use during the winter to protect your alloys from damp and salt.

If your car starts vibrating at around 65mph (100kph), check the tyre pressures. The MX-5 is very sensitive to tyre pressures, and the car will be happiest with 28psi at each corner.

Vibration can also be caused by a stiff spot on the tyre where the belts inside the tyre carcass overlap. Try a tyre with a jointless nylon band, and have wheels balanced to 1/10 of a gram.

These problems are most likely to affect cars made before the chassis was stiffened in 1994.

To keep your car handling crisply, the shock absorbers should be changed every 30,000 miles. However, some aftermarket items last longer or even offer a lifetime guarantee.

Mechanical

Make sure the oil is changed every 3,000–5,000 miles (5–8,000km), and opt for a synthetic.

HT leads usually only last 30,000 miles (48,000km). If you have any kind of misfire, the leads should be the prime suspect.

Mk1s have a small battery in the right-hand side of its boot, which goes flat very easily, so make sure you don't leave the lights on, even for a couple of hours.

The Miata loves to be driven, and hates to stand for long periods. If you don't drive your Mk1 regularly the clutch will get squeaky, the battery can go flat and the spark plugs can flood when you fire it up again.

The throttle body can get gummed up with black oil

The Mk1 battery can go flat very easily so make sure you don't leave your lights on. (James Mann)

Accessory trolleys or an in-garage hoist will keep your hard-top in top-notch condition. (James Mann)

Inside the cabin

If your leather seats are looking tired and dried up, UK club members recommend the leather restoration kit offered by Woolies of Market Deeping, near Peterborough (Tel. 01778 347347).

Use the air-conditioning regularly to keep it healthy. If you are inspecting a car you want to buy and it has air-conditioning, check that it produces a fridge-like blast for a couple of minutes with the vents set to recirculating.

The engine revs should change as the air-con is switched on, indicating that the pump is working.

Cars usually need recharging every seven to 10 years because of leaks in the system. Regular use will extend the time between recharges.

Hoods

It is essential to zip out the Mk1's plastic window before folding the roof window, or it will become folded and creased. The correct method is to unlatch the top, unzip the window and lower it. The reverse procedure is to put up the top, zip in the rear window and then latch the top. This takes the strain off the zip, otherwise you may find the teeth coming loose.

It is a good idea, too, to check the zip for fraying or any loose threads where the teeth are stitched on to the backing, as this can sometimes foul the zip and jam it.

If you regularly drive roof-down without fitting the tonneau, the exposed underside of the roof can become dried out, damaged by hot sun, or it may go mouldy after a sudden shower of rain.

In the winter, scraping ice off the plastic window will scratch it, using warm water is a much kinder option.

Mild fogginess and minor scratches on the rear window can be cured with Meguiars Plastic Polish (available through the UK club).

The hard-top is very easy to put on but you need somewhere safe to store it. Accessory companies, including Moss offer a trolley to move it, or you can have a hoist inside your garage.

deposits. These should be removed gently with mineral spirits or carburettor cleaner. However, be careful not to clean off the coating Mazda put inside the bore to assist the blade seating, otherwise you'll suffer leaks, rough idling and poor driveability.

Treat your transmission to a synthetic transmission oil made by a well known name such as Redline, Mobil or Amsoil. Make sure it meets the API service GL-4 or GL-5 rating.

Inspired sensation by Tom Matano

In 1984, I created this story to express our philosophy …

A car starts to draw more attention than another, either it passes you on a freeway, or you see it for a split second on a TV screen. It makes you want to find out what it is.

You start to develop some expectations about how it feels to drive, how you look in it, or the lifestyle you may lead with it. After a while, you discover that it was a Miata.

Then you may want to go to the dealership for a closer look. Upon closer inspection, you are satisfied that your expectations and excitement were justified.

You open the door, and the sight of the interior is so inviting, that you can't help but sit in it. From the first turn of the key, the engine starts, and it sounds and feels exactly how you imagined it would.

The first turn of the wheel … how it corners, and the way it stops. The car goes beyond initial expectations.

By the end of the test drive, we would like you to become a Mazda owner …

In the past, our product development efforts ended at that very moment. However, our new philosophy really begins here. We went on describing the type of life our customer would lead after the purchase.

The customer takes the car home, and, of course, takes the family for a ride, shows it to their neighbours and friends. Just before retiring to bed, you stop for one last look, and even say 'goodnight' to the car, or maybe even sit in the car one last time.

On your daily route, you start to think about more challenging roads … Or new routes in order to spend more time with the car.

On your first out-of-town trip, you discover other aspects of the car's personality that you didn't realise from your daily routine. You discover the depth of the car more and more, as days, months, and years go by.

Of course, even with the most prolonged driver-car relationship, there comes a time when the owner has to part with the car. You part with fond memories, which you will treasure for a long, long time.

And further down the road, the customer seeks out and finds the same model, buys it again and restores it.

Miata was the first product developed under this philosophy, and all the other Mazda cars that followed were products of this philosophy.

Tom's signature on a bootlid. (Andrew Fearon)

Appendix B

Specifications and performance figures

1990

Mazda MX-5 1.6

Engine	In-line 4-cylinder, water-cooled, DOHC, 16 valves, longitudinal
Displacement	1,598cc
Bore x stroke	78 x 83.6mm
Max power	114bhp @ 6,500rpm
Max torque	100lb ft @ 5,500rpm
Compression ratio	9.4:1
Induction system	Electronic fuel injection
Cylinder block	Cast iron
Cylinder head	Die-cast aluminium
Fuel tank	45 litres (9.9gal)
Fuel	Unleaded (min 91 ON)
Transmission	Five-speed manual
Gear ratios	1st – 3.136
	2nd – 1.888
	3rd – 1.330
	4th – 1.000
	5th – 0.814
	Rev – 3.758
Final gear ratio	4.300
Clutch	Hydraulically operated single dry plate, diaphragm spring
Diameter	200mm (7.87in)
Steering	Rack and pinion, power-assisted
Turns lock-to-lock	2.8
Turning circle	9.14m (29.99ft)
Brakes (front)	236mm (9.29in) ventilated disc
Brakes (rear)	231mm (9.09in) solid disc
Disc thickness	Front – 18mm (0.71in)
	Rear – 9mm (0.35in)
Vacuum servo	8in
Parking brake	Mechanical on rear wheels
Chassis and suspension	Body monocoque

Suspension (front)	Independent by double wishbone and coil spring
Suspension (rear)	Independent by double wishbone and coil spring
Shock absorbers (front)	Cylindrical double-acting, gas-filled
Shock absorbers (rear)	Cylindrical double-acting, gas-filled
Stabiliser	Torsion bar
Tyres	Dunlop P185/60 R14 82H steel radial
Wheel size	5.5JJ x 14
Wheel material	Aluminium alloy
Spare wheel	Space-saver
Dimensions (external)	
Length	3,975mm (156.5in)
Width	1,675mm (65.9in)
Height	1,230mm (48.4in)
Wheelbase	2,265mm (89.1in)
Track (front)	1,410mm (55.5in)
Track (rear)	1,430mm (56.3in)
Ground clearance (laden)	115mm (4.5in)
Dimensions (internal)	
Front legroom	1,085mm (42.7in)
Headroom (top closed)	942mm (37.0in)
Shoulder room	1,280mm (50.3in)
Kerb weight	995kg (2,193lb)
Weight distribution	52:48 f/r unladen
Towing capacity	
Braked trailer	700kg
Unbraked trailer	350kg
Performance (per Mazda Motor Corporation)	
Max speed	121mph (195kph)
0–62mph (96.5kph)	8.75sec
Fuel consumption	Urban – 29.4mpg (9.6l/100km)
	56mph (90kph) – 46.3mpg (6.1l/100km)
	75mph (121kph) – 36.2mpg (7.8l/100km)

Standard equipment	Momo leather steering wheel
	Power-assisted steering
	Electric windows
	Tachometer
	Sun visors with passenger vanity mirror
	Clarion CRH60 stereo radio/cassette (detachable front)
	Manual aerial
	Front door speakers
	Lockable central storage box
Colours (UK)	Classic Red
	Mariner Blue
	Crystal White
	Silver Stone metallic
Interior	Black cloth

July 1993

Mazda MX-5 1.8i (replaces 1.6i)

Engine	(1.8 from Mazda 323F GT) In-line 4-cylinder, water-cooled, DOHC, 16 valves, longitudinal
Displacement	1,839cc
Bore x stroke	78 x 83.6mm
Max power	128bhp @ 6,500rpm
Max torque	110lb ft @ 5,000rpm
Compression ratio	9.0:1
Camshafts	Hollow, for lighter weight
Induction system	Electronic fuel injection
Cylinder block	Cast iron
Cylinder head	Die-cast aluminium
Fuel tank	45 litres (9.9gal)
Fuel	Unleaded (min 91 ON)
Transmission	Final drive ratio 4.10:1
Brakes (front)	254mm ventilated discs
Brakes (rear)	251mm solid discs (Larger diameter from 1994)
Chassis	Body shell stiffened. Steel rod between front suspension assemblies, stiffer rear anti-roll bars, brace between seatbelt anchor points behind the driver
Suspension	Stiffer springs and brushes, Bilstein sports damper, thicker anti-roll bar from 1994
Tyres	Pirelli P700-Z tyres available from December 1993
Wheels	Seven-spoke alloy
Wheel size	6 x 14in standard on 1.8 models from 1994
Kerb weight	1,020kg (2,249lb)
Weight distribution	51/49 f/r unladen

Interior	Seats with separate headrest replace those with integral items
	Passenger airbag available

Performance (Mazda Motor Corporation)

Max speed	120mph – 193kph
	0–60mph – (96.5kph) 8.5sec
Fuel consumption	Urban – 22mpg (13l/100km)
	Motorway – 27mpg (10.5l/100km)
Standard Equipment	Momo leather steering wheel
	Power-assisted steering
	Electric windows
	Tachometer
	Sun visors with passenger vanity mirror
	Clarion CRH60 stereo radio/cassette (detachable front)
	Manual aerial
	Front door speakers
	Lockable central storage box
	Electrically adjustable mirrors
	Electric aerial
	ABS optional
	Alarm optional

1995

1.8i

Engine	Flywheel lightened to make engine more free-revving. From August, 133bhp standardised worldwide
Final drive	4.3:1 optional for those wanting acceleration rather than a higher top speed, became standard from 1995

BBS 6J x 15in alloy wheels with P195/55 HR15 tyres offered as an option. Recaro seats become optional

1.6i

Reintroduced with 88bhp to widen gap with 1.8

1996

Rear badges become green
Dials lose chrome surrounds

1997

Spring, high-level brake light added to bootlid

1998

Mk2

	1.6i	1.8i
Engine In-line 4-cylinder		
Displacement	1,597cc	1,839cc
Max power @ 6,500rpm	108bhp	140bhp
Max torque @ 5,000rpm	99lb ft	119lb ft
Specific output	68bhp per litre	
Power-to-weight, per tonne	108bhp	136bhp
Bore and stroke	78 x 83.6mm	83 x 85mm
Compression ratio	9.4:1	9.5:1

Gearbox	Five-speed
Gear ratios	1st – 31.4
	2nd – 1.89
	3rd – 1.33
	4th – 1.00
	5th – 0.81
	Final drive – 4.10

Tyres	1.6i – Yokohama A-460 185/60 HR14
	1.8i – Michelin Pilot 195/50VR15 SX GT
Tyre size	5.5J x 14in
Wheels	Cast alloy
Spare wheel	Space-saver

Dimensions (external)

Length	3,975mm (156.5in)
Width	1,680mm (66.1in)
Height	1,225mm (48.2in)
Wheelbase	2,265mm (89.2in)

Dimensions (internal)

Headroom	942mm (37.0in)
Legroom	1,086mm (42.8in)
Shoulder room	1,263mm (49.7in)

Kerb weight	2,255lb (1,025kg)
Weight distribution	50/50 f/r unladen

Performance

Max speed	1.6i – 119mph (191kph)
	1.8i – 126mph (203kph)
0–60mph (96.5kph)	1.6i – 9.7sec
	1.8i – 7.8sec *(Autocar)*

Fuel consumption	Urban – 26.7mpg (10.6l/100km)
	Extra urban – 42.8mpg (6.6l/100km)
	Combined – 34.9mpg (8.1l/100km)

Standard equipment	Driver and passenger airbags, power steering
Optional equipment	Metallic paint, air-conditioning, wind blocker, hard-top

ABS not available

1.8iS

Adds anti-lock brakes, seatbelt tensioners, central locking

Mk2 1.8 10th Anniversary

Engine	In-line 4-cylinder
Displacement	1,839cc
Max power	140bhp @ 6,500rpm
Max torque	119lb ft @ 4,500rpm

Gearbox	Manual six-speed
Gear ratios	1st – 3.760
	2nd – 2.269
	3rd – 1.645
	4th – 1.257
	5th – 1.000
	6th – 0.843
	Rev – 3.564
	Final drive – 3.636

Performance

Max speed	126mph (203kph)
0–62mph (100kph)	8.4sec

Fuel consumption	Urban cycle – 24.1mpg (11.7l/100km)
	Extra urban – 39.8mpg (7.1l/100km)
	Combined – 32.1mpg (8.8l/100km)

Mk3

Engine	In-line 4-cylinder, aluminium alloy, DOHC with sequential valve timing			
Size	1.6i	1.8i	1.8i Auto	1.8i Sport 6sp
Displacement	1,597cc	1,839cc	1,839cc	1,839cc
Max power	110bhp	146bhp	139bhp	145bhp
	@ 6,500rpm	@ 7,000rpm	@ 6,500rpm	@ 7,000rpm
Max torque				
@5,000rpm	99lb ft	124lb ft	125lb ft	124lb ft
Max speed	119mph	127mph	118mph	129mph
0–62mph (100kph)	9.7sec	8.5sec	11.0sec	8.4sec
Fuel consumption	34.9mpg	32.5mpg	29.8mpg	31.7mpg
Weight	1,100kg (2,425lb)			
Power-to-weight	133bhp/tonne			

Standard equipment	Driver and passenger airbags with passenger seat airbag deactivation system
	Seatbelt pretensioners
	Power door locks
	Electric windows
	Anti-lock brakes with EBD (electronic brake-force distribution)
	Alarm
	Immobiliser

1.8i Sport

Adds leather trim, leather-wrap gearknob and Nardi steering wheel, remote central locking with boot release, power door mirrors, electric aerial, radio and single CD player.

Great websites

World community

Australian MX-5 Turbo: www.mazda.com.au
Check out details of MX-5 SP on Mazda
Australia's official site.

www.MiataClubs.com
A virtual club

**Cruzin' Chris:
www.geocities.com/MotorCity/5361**
Details of Miatas in America by Chris Lambert,
giving colours, comments and spotting tips. If
you can't find him in the geocities maze, look up
Lamberts's Home Page in your search engine.

Flyin' Miata: www.flyin.miata.com
What the performance-crazy boys are up to; the
current racing car, plus details of parts offered
for sale.

**Kanazawa Roadster Club of Japan:
www.roadster.hotspace.jp**
Lively site showing what's going on in Japan,
pictures of members' cars and reviews of mods
and accessories. Click option for English language.

Ka Yu Autos: www.kayuautos.com
Step-by-step instructions for simple
modifications such as changing the air filter and
timing, plus maintenance checks.

Miata.net: www.miata.net
The essential address for the MX-5/Miata
community, with all the news. 'Ask Bob!' section
allows you to put questions direct to Bob Hall.
Lots of useful sections including
Miata.net/garage, plus links to hundreds of
individual websites, including Keith Tanner from
Flyin' Miata (NB the Ice Racer is a joke) and Mike
Hayward of UK owners' club. Or you can put up
your own site.

**Miata Owners' Club (USA):
www.miataownersclub.com**

Miata Ring: www.miata.net/ring
A ring of websites – keep going and you come
back to the Home Page. Register and request
information.

Modifications: www.miata.org/cmt/bsp
Some wild mods to give you ideas.

**MX-5 Owners' Club Australia:
www.MX5.com.au**
Offers links to all the different state chapters.

MX-5 Owners' Club UK: www.mx5oc.co.uk
Run by membership secretary, Mike Hayward,
excellent site offering masses of information,
advice and links. Eunos owners should check out
the link to Les's Roadster Pages.

**MX-5 Owners' Club New Zealand:
www.mx5club.org.nz**
Lots of pics of reports of what the club has been
up to, plus Q&A section.

**Bob Moore's MX-5 addicts page:
www.mooremvp.freeserve.co.uk**
A keen owner gives reviews of models and links
to other useful sites.

Nitrous injection: www.n2omx5.com
What is it? How does it work? How easy it is to fit?

**or www.mongrelms.homestead.com/
mx5nitrous**
Mongrel Motorsport's website.

Overboost: www.overboost.com
Company site includes features about
performance mods and specialist companies.

Racing Beat: www.racingbeat.com
Clear pictures and information on products and
radical project cars.

**Roadster Club of Japan: www.open-
inc.co.jp/rcoj**
Not strictly a great website for westerners
because it's mainly in Japanese.
e-mail: rcoj@open-inc.co.jp

V8 power: www.v8miata.com
Panache site by Martin Wilson, includes photos,
figures and details of V8 conversion kit.

**V8-powered Australian special:
www.bulletcars.com**
Bullet is now owned by Advanced Engine
Components Ltd. Details of Bullet and other
conversions.

Sport

Autocross: www.autocross.com

www.drive2race.com
For all those who enjoy autocross, time trials
and racing.

**Good Win Racing: www.good-win-
racing.com**

**John McCormack's 1991 Racing Eunos Roadster:
www.car.carecentre.co.uk/racing**

**Mazda Sport Cup 2001:
www.astraracing.com**
Information on the European one-make race
series and the tuning company which prepares
the cars, Astra Racing. Sadly, for us, most of the
site is in Italian.

www.miataracing.net
Site dedicated to SCCA Miata racing in the USA.

**Miata Spec racing (USA):
www.prospecmiata.com**

**Solo Miata preparation:
www.members.aol.com/solomiata**
Tips and instructions to prepare your car and boost
its power, including engine swap, 1.8 into 1.6.

**Sports Car Club of America (SCCA):
www.scca.org**

Or, www.wtrsscca.org/tech gives details of
the rule book for competitors to buy, with e-mail
link.

Appendix D

Parts, accessories and services

The following addresses and telephone/fax numbers were believed correct at the time of going to press. However, as these are subject to change, particularly area dialling codes, no guarantee can be given for their continuing accuracy.

ADDCO MANUFACTURING CO. INTERNATIONAL
1596 Linville Falls Hwy, Linville NC 28646
Tel. 1-800 338 7015
Website: www.addco.net
E-mail: sales@addco.net
Performance handling parts, sway bars and suspension kits.

APEX AUTOMOTIVE ENGINEERING
667 Farm Rd, Marlborough, MA 01752
Tel. (508) 229-0090
E-mail: apex@miata.net
Repairs and performance.

AUTOHOODS LTD
Chessington, Surrey
Tel. (0)20 8391 5324
Website: www.autohoods.co.uk
E-mail: Info@autohoods.co.uk
Replacement soft-tops.

AUTOSUPERMART.COM
28 Overlook Farms, Killingworth, CT 06419
Tel. 203-752-9662
Accessories.

AUTOPOWER INDUSTRIES
Tel. 619 297-3300
Fax 619 297-9765
Aftermarket.

AUTOTECH DESIGN LTD
Tel. +44 (0) 20 8661 8999
Burr walnut, carbon fibre, brushed aluminium or pearl alloy console trim, plus body kits and accessories.

AUTOTRIM SYSTEMS
Wesle Street, Leicester LE4 5QG
Tel. +44 (0) 116 266 4112
Fax +44 (0) 116 265 0652
Hoods, leather seats, upholstery repairs, hard-top covers.

AUTOTHORITY
3769-B Pickett Road, Fairfax, VA 22031
Tel. 800-286-9075
Performance chips.

BRG
Bourne Road Garage Limited, Bourne Road, Crayford, Kent DA1 4BU
Tel. 01322 521595
MX-5 specialist. Excellent website: www.mx5-mazda.co.uk/MX5 – features special editions catalogues with details of each model and displays original brochures. Will put you on waiting list for a particular car. Also sells parts and factory hard-tops.

BRITISH TRIM CO
Tel. 01633 423976
Brambles, Catash Road, Christchurch, Newport, South Wales UK NP18 1JJ
Hoods, hood envolopes, tonneaus, leather seats covers, gearstick gaiters and handbrake gaiters.

BRODIE BRITTAIN RACING (BBR)
Oxford Road, Brackley, Northants NN13 5DY UK
Tel. 01280 702 389
Fax 01280 705 339
Turbocharging; creators of the original MX-5 BBR Turbo.

BAUMGARTNER, BRANDT, AND SHILTACH (BBS)
5320 BBS Drive, Braselton, Georgia 30517
Tel. 800-422-7972 and 770-967-9848
Wheels manufacturer.

BELL ENGINEERING GROUP, INC (BEGI)
11723 Warfield, San Antonio, TX 78216
Tel. 210-349-6515
Turbochargers/superchargers.

BILSTEIN CORPORATION OF AMERICA
8845 Rehco Road, San Diego, CA 92121
Tel. 619-453-7723
Shock absorbers.

BORLA PERFORMANCE INDUSTRIES
5901 Edison Drive, Oxnard, CA 93033
Tel. 805-986-8600
Fax 805-986-8999
Aftermarket exhausts.

BR PERFORMANCE
403-E Miller Road, Greenville, SC 29607
Tel. 864-963-8286
Fax (520) 447-6261
E-mail: br@brperformance.net
Aftermarket.

BRAINSTORM PRODUCTS
Website: www.miata.org/cmt/bsp
2608 S La Cienega Blvd, LA CA90034
Tech line Tel. 310-815-9825
Fax 310-815-9854
Order line Tel. 800-779-3223
Visual mods such as BSP low-profile twin headlamps, chin spoiler, moulded armrest, sport grille, chrome details, brushed aluminium dash inserts, performance exhausts, uprated suspension.

BRIDGESTONE TIRES
1 Bridgestone Place, Nashville, TN 37214
Tel. 615-391-0088
Tyres.

CABRIO WORLD
396 Littleton Ave, Newark, NJ 07103
Tel. 800-752-1563 and 973-642-2404
Fax 603-309-7761
E-mail: info@cabrioworld.com
Hoods.

CAMDEN SUPERCHARGERS
16715 Meridian East Bldg K-A, Puyallup WA
98375
Superchargers.

CARTECH
11723 Warfield, San Antonio, TX 78216
Tel. 210-308-8464
Turbochargers.

CHES CAIN AMSOIL INDEPENDENT DEALER
2334 Highwood Dr, Dallas, Tx 75228
Tel. and Fax 214-324-4998

CLASSIC ADDITIONS
Stert, Devizes, Wiltshire SN10 3JD
Website: www.classicadditions.co.uk
Tel. 01380 720419/720970
Wind deflectors and car covers.

CLASSIC MOTORING ACCESSORIES, LTD.
5008 West Linebaugh Ave, Suite 60 Tampa,
Florida 33624
Tel. 813-968-7596
Fax 813-960-9512
E-mail: classic1@tampabay.rr.com

CLASSIC MOTORBOOKS
PO Box 1 Osceola, WI 54020
Tel. 800-826-6600/715-294-3345
Fax 715-294-4448

CLEARWATER
PO Box 428 Folsom, CA 95763
Tel. 916-983-6162
Fax 916-983-4205
Aftermarket audio.

CONCEPT VEHICLE RESTORATIONS
Unit 2, Mayland Ind Est, Steeple Road, Mayland,
Essex CM3 6AX
Tel. 0621 744772
Leather seats – recommended by members of
the UK MX-5 Owners' Club.

CRAZY RED ITALIAN
8161-B Belvedere Ave Sacramento, CA 95826
Tel. 800-412-7299
Int. tel. 916-456-2277
E-mail: crazyred@miata.net
Air horns.

DAYTONA INT. TRADING CO.
Tel. 538-35-6111 Fax 538-37-0809
Aftermarket supplier in Japan.

DISCOUNT TIRE DIRECT
7333 E. Helms Drive, Suite No. 7 Scottsdale, AZ
85260
Tel. 800-790-6444
Fax 602-443-5621
Tyres.

DONUTZ
1 Beech Lees, Farsley, Pudsey, West Yorkshire
LS28 5JY
Website: www.donutz.co.uk
UK-based company, sells solely from the net;
huge variety of visual mods for body and cabin,
plus dual headlamps, performance exhausts and
suspension kits. Imports popular items from the
USA, including BrainStorm, Team Voodoo
aluminium gearknobs etc. Also, Matt Clark glass
rear windows.

DUETTO MOTORS LLC
21740 Devonshire Street, Chatsworth, CA 91311
Website: www.flashnet/~duetto/catalog.htm
Tel. 818-727-0969 Fax 818-727-9195
E-mail: duetto@flash.net
Tops and aftermarket accessories.

DUNLOP TYRE COMPANY
PO Box 1109 Buffalo, NY 14240-1109
Tel. 800-828-7428
Fax 716-639-5200
Tyres.

ENHANCED PERFORMANCE
1111 N. William St, Goldsboro, NC 27530
Tel. 919-580-9016

ENTHUZA CAR
12195 Hwy 92, Suite 114 No. 325, Woodstock,
GA 30188-3603
Tel. 770-928-9521
Fax 770-928-1782

EREBUNI CORP
Website: www.erebuni.net
E-mail: info@eribunicorp.com
Eribuni Corp, 158 Roebling St, Brooklyn NY 11211
Tel. 718 387 0800
Fax 718 486 7957
Suppliers of wings, spoilers and full body kits.

EURASIAN PARTS SELECT
Tel. 800-824-8814 and 909-308-1745
Fax 909-308-1751
Aftermarket.

EUNOSVERSE
Website: www.eunosverse.com
Tel. 0800 026 5594 (UK)
Parts and accessories for MX-5 and Eunos
Roadster.

PETER FARRELL SUPERCARS
9208-B Venture Court, Manassas, VA 22111
Tel. 703-368-6947
Fax 703-368-1201

FINISH LINE PERFORMANCE
615 Carlisle Drive, Herndon, VA 20170
Tel. 1-888-450-3220
Int. tel. 703-796-6671
E-mail: info@finishlineperformance.com
Aftermarket.

FITTIPALDI MOTORING ACCESSORIES
1425 NW 82nd Avenue, Miami, FL 33126
Tel. 305-592-8177
Wheels.

FLYIN' MIATA (FORMERLY DEALER
ALTERNATIVE)
331 South 13th Street, Grand Junction, CO 81501
Website: www.flyinmiata.com
E-mail: info@dlralt.com
Tech line Tel. 970-242-3800
Fax 970-242-9199
Order line: 1-800-FLY-MX5S
Turbocharging, and designs own suspension kits.
Eight different types of exhausts, larger brake
kits, fully programmable replacement engine
computers, performance accessories, Dynojet
dyno tuning.

GOOD-WIN RACING
927 Wilbur Ave. No. 3, San Diego, CA 92109
Website: www.good-win-racing.com

GRASSROOTS MOTORSPORTS
555 W Granada, Suite B9, Ormond Beach, FL,
32174
Tel. 904-673-6148
Fax 904-673-6040
E-mail: GRMPer@aol.com

HKS
20312 Gramercy Place, Torrance, CA 90501
Tel. 310-328-8100
Fax 310-618-6911
US branch of Japanese performance parts
specialist.

HARD DOG FABRICATION
Tel. 800-688-9652 and 910-922-3018
Roll bars.

HOLLEY
Website: www.holley.com
Nitrous-oxide conversion kit supplier.

HOODS GALORE UK
Website: www.hoodsgalore.com
Tel. 020 8665 6355
Hoods made in Germany to original specification.

HYPERSPEED, INC.
5403 West Crenshaw Street, Tampa, FL 33634
Tel. 813-685-7342
Fax 813-888-9893
Aftermarket.

IL MOTORSPORT
Esserstrasse 24, 50354 Efferen, Germany
Tel. 02233/977349 and 78471
Fax 02233/977348
Aftermarket accessories and performance parts.

IMPARTS LTD
Tel. 800-325-9043
Fax 800-525-9043
Aftermarket.

JACKSON RACING
7281 Westminster, Westminster, CA 92683
Tel. 714-891-1113
Fax 714-895-6873
Aftermarket.

JACKSON RACING SUPERCHARGER
440 Rutherford St, Golita CA93117
Tel. 888-888-4079 toll free USA, and 805-681-
3410
Fax 805-692-2523
E-mail: jacksonracing@mossmotors.com
Performance parts and supercharging kit. (See
also Moss.)

JAG BAGS
37 Highwood Avenue, Solihull, West Midlands
B92 8QY
Website: www.jagbags.co.uk
Tel. 0121 743 8646
Rear parcel shelf travel bags, spare wheel
storage bag for Mk1, hood cover bag, rear
window protector, luggage sets designed to fit
precisely into the boot.

J&B
4520 Schoolway Drive, Greensboro, NC 27406
Tel. 910-674-3970
Aftermarket.

JOHNSON COMPANY
PO Box 303 Lincoln Park, NJ 07035
Tel. 1-800-323-3045
Int. tel. 201-633-3933
Fax 201-633-0566
E-mail: info@autotops.com
Robbins convertible tops.

KA YU AUTO PARTS
3 Black Bank, Exhall, Coventry CV7 9NX UK
Website: www.kayuautos.com
E-mail: kayuautos@msn.com
Tel. 024 7631 8729
Parts and accessories for Mazda and Eunos, also
imports cars.

K&N ENGINEERING
PO Box 1329 Riverside, CA 92502
Tel. 714-684-9762 and 1-800-858-3333
Aftermarket air systems.

KEW WEST LONDON LTD
Website: www.kewwest.com
Tel. 0208 392 9244
MX-5 specialist, car sales, servicing and repairs,
security equipment.

KG WORKS
Sugeta-Cho 2737 Kanagawa-Ku, Yokohama-City
Kanagawa-Pref
Japan
Tel. 045-471-2841
Fax 045-472-9013
Website: www.kgworks.co.jp/eng/main-e.htm
E-mail info@kgworks.co.jp
Wild visual mods, including a Ferrari-style gear
lever gate. See Scole Engineering, UK.

KNOBMEISTER
7851 South Logan Street, Littleton, CO 80122-
2810
Tel. 303-730-6060
Fax 303-730-6425
E-mail: qualityimages@miata.net

LAV ENTERPRISES
Tel. 708-438-0568
Aftermarket audio.

LEWIS MARKETING
30 Alania Place, Kihei Maui, Hi. 96753
Lumbar supports.

LUSSO CAR CARE PRODUCTS
63 Oak Street, Norwood, NJ 07648
Tel. 1-800-851-2737
E-mail:sales@lusso.com
Car care.

LV ENGINEERING
11 West Hampstead Mews, London NW8 3BB
Website: www.lvengineering.com
Tel. 0207 624 4588

MM MARKETING
Fayetteville, NC
E-mail: info@mmmiata.com
Tel. 910-323-8773; 800-666-4282 Fax 910-323-
4272
Aftermarket accessories.

MROAD
1779 Wells Branch Pkwy No. 110B PMB 330
Austin, TX 78728
E-mail: info@mroad.com
Tel. 512-695-7432
Fax 603-697-6336
Body stripes, tops, roll bars, exhausts.

MARIAH MOTORSPORTS
Tel. 805-965-5115
Fax 805-965-5332
Service.

MATT DEVELOPMENTS
Unit B6, Hastingswood Trading Estate, Harbet
Road, London N18 3LP
Tel. 0208 803 1122
Website: www.mattdevelopments.co.uk
E-mail: Matt@mattdevelopments.co.uk
Glass rear screen conversion kit for Mk1 hoods,
easy-lift gas strut system for all MX-5 hood
frames.

MAZ-ALL
790 Indian Trail Rd Ste B101 Lilburn, Ga 30047
Tel. 678-924-7603
Repairs and performance.

MAZBAGZ!
Website: www.mazbagz.co.uk
Tel. 0800 0155532
Luggage sets for MX-5.

MAZMART, INC.
4917 New Peachtree Road Atlanta, GA 30341-
3122
E-mail: info@mazmart.com
Tel. 800-221-5156
Local tel. 770-455-4848
Fax 770-451-1999
Mazda Recycling

MAZDA AUTO RECYCLING
3450 Recycle Road Rancho Cordova, CA 95742
Tel. 800-926-5900
Used parts.

MAZDA COMPETITION PARTS
Tel. 800-435-2508
Fax 714-454-7157
Aftermarket; membership required.

MAZDAFORMANCE
c/o JLH Automotive 1011 Sherwood Forest Drive
Houston, TX 77043
Tel. 800-233-2991
E-mail: support@mazdaformance.com
Aftermarket and dealership.

THE MAZDA MX-5 SHOP
Milestone House, Penrith Cumbria
Tel. 01768 866586
Website: www.northerntr.freeserve.co.uk
Club sports specialists: cars prepared for track
or competition, new and used spares,
accessories, blue-printed engines.

MAZDA SOUTH
Roger Beasley Mazda South, 4506 S. IH-35
Austin, TX 78745
Tel. 877-96-SOUTH
Aftermarket and dealership.

MAZTEK
Unit 27, Ketley Business Park, Waterloo Road,
Ketley, Telford, Shropshire TF1 5JD
Tel. 01952 244266
Performance parts and tuning, supercharging or
turbocharging, service.

METROTEC
1152 Birch Dr, Petaluma, CA 94952
Tel. 707-778-8999

MIATA MAGAZINE
1315 Buena Vista Drive Vista, CA 92083
E-mail Barb@MiataMagazine.com
Tel. (760) 631-7474 FAX (760) 631-1206

MIGHTY PRODUCTS
6376 Foster Street, Palm Beach Gardens,
FL 33418
Tel. 800-76-Miata and 407-744-7238
Aftermarket.

MODERN PERFORMANCE
Website: www.modernperformance.com
Tel. 713 270 8520; toll free (USA) 877-247-6366
Exhaust systems and performance parts.

MOMO USA
2100 N.W. 93rd Avenue, Miami, FL 33172
Tel. 305 593 0493 and 305 593 1937

MONSTER MOTORSPORTS
2312 Vineyard Avenue, Escondido, CA 92029
Tel. 619-738-7592
Fax 760-738-7593
Creators of the V8-engined Monster Miata and
supercharged V8 Mega-Monster.

MOSS EUROPE
Website: www.moss-europe.co.uk
Massive range of parts and accessories
including steering wheels, dual headlamp
conversion, replacement hoods, wheels and
tyres, interior styling items and performance and
handling parts.

MOSS MOTORS
7200 Hollister Avenue PO Box 847, Goleta, CA
93116
Tel. 800-235-6959, 800-642-8295 or
805-968-1041
Fax 805-968-6910

MOTORSPORT
1139 W. Collins Avenue, Orange, CA 92667
Tel. 800-633-6331, 714 639 2620 and 714 639
7460
Aftermarket.

MX-5 OWNERS CLUB REGALIA (UK)
Colin Frewer, 14 Cobham Way, Merley,
Wimborne, Dorset BH21 1 SJ
Tel. 01202 885034
Clothing and caps embroidered with your choice
of MX5 logo; keys rings and more.

MX5PARTS.CO.UK
Unit 4, Cluster Industrial Estate, Rodney Road,
Portsmouth, Hampshire PO4 8ST
Tel. 0845 345 2384
Specialist in parts for all MX-5 and Eunos
Roadsters, ordered online.

NARDI USA
5320 BBS Drive, Braselton, GA 30517
Tel. 800-826-2734 and 770-967-9817
Fax 770-967-9866
Steering wheels, etc.

NELSON SUPERCHARGERS
3724 Overland Avenue, Los Angeles, CA 90034
Tel. 310-204-0126/7/8
Fax 310-204-5171

OVERBOOST
Website: www.overboost.com
Tel. 877 HI BOOST and 011 1 626 358 4660 for
overseas orders.

OZ WHEELS
1435 NW 82nd Avenue, Miami, FL 33126
Tel. 305-594-1882
Fax 305-592-5186

PANACHE
382 Enterprise St, Suite 108, San Marcos, CA
92069 Tel. 760 510 9682
E-mail Martinv8@junocom
V8 conversions.

PBC (PERFORMANCE BUYERS CLUB)
14620C Flint Lee Road, Chantilly, VA 21051
Tel.800-359-4093 (info, orders, customer
support) and 703-818-9840
E-mail: info@performancebuyers.com

PROMOTEX ONLINE
c/o Box 184, Neche ND 58265 USA
Models.

RACING BEAT
1291 Hancock Street, Anaheim, CA 92807
Website: www.racingbeat.com
Tel. 714-779-8677
Fax 714-779-2902
Performance-boosting parts including exhaust
systems, high-flow intake manifolds, suspension
packages, style bars.

RED LINE OIL COMPANY
3450 Pacheco Blvd. Martinez, CA 94553
Tel. 800-624-7958 and 510 228 7576

ROADSTER PERFORMANCE
5808 Solitude Way, Durham, NC 27713
Tel. 919-484-4100
Aftermarket.

ROBERT'S MIATA PRODUCTS
12814 South 40th Place Phoenix, AZ 85044
Tel. and Fax 480-753-9377
Aftermarket.

ROBBINS AUTO TOP COMPANY
711 Olympic Blvd, Santa Monica, CA 90401
Tel. 310-450-3444
Fax 310-452-0563
Soft-tops.

RONAL USA
15692 Computer Lane, Huntington Beach, CA
92649-1608
Tel. 800-899-1212 and 714-891-4853
Fax 714-897-5611
Wheels.

RSPEED
Website: www.rspeed.net
1011 South Marietta Parkway, Suite 4, Marietta,
GA 30060
Tel. 888-551-0025 and 678-290-7504
Fax 678-290-7535
E-mail: questions@rspeed.net
Parts from Germany and IL Motorsport.

RX HEAVEN LTD
Edmonton, Alberta
Tel. 403-430-0783
Fax 403-430-0783
Aftermarket.

SCCA (SPORTS CAR CLUB OF AMERICA)
9033 E Easter Place, Centennial, CO 80112
Website: www.scca.org
Tel. 303-694-7222, toll free (USA) 800-770-2055
Fax 303-694-7391

SCIMITAR INTERNATIONAL MX5 PARTS
4 Cluster Industrial Estate, Rodney Road,
Portsmouth, Hampshire PO4 8ST
Website: www.MX5parts.co.uk
Tel. 0845-345-2384
Enormous range of visual enhancements
including bodykits, chrome details and coloured
or luminescent dial faces, replacement hoods,
performance exhausts and air intakes,
suspension kits.

SCOLE ENGINEERING
Norfolk, UK
E-mail: Scoleng@aol.com
Tel. 01379 740940
KG Works accessories, including Ferrari-style
gate, mesh grille, metal console inserts; power
boosting kits and rolling road to record the boost
in bhp.

SEAT SURGEONS LTD
Tel. 0208 661 8999
Leather trim, dashboard sets, gearknobs.

SEBRING SUPERCHARGERS
7200 Hollister Avenue, PO Box 847, Goleta,
CA 93116
Tel. 800-235-6959, 800-642-8295 and
805-968-1041
Fax 805-968-6910

SERIOUS AUTOMOTIVE ACCESSORIES
5020 Soquel Drive, Soquel, CA 95073
Tel. 408-475-5722
Fax 408-336-2108
Website: www.seriousauto.zoovy.com
Performance parts, visual mods, seats,
suspension kits, soft-tops, tonneaus, Hard Dog
roll-over bars, Oris windstop, also organises
events.

SPORTS & CLASSIC SOLUTIONS
Tel. +44 (0)1234 871499
E-mail: Sales@sandcs.com
Borla exhausts, ceramic headers, front and rear
roll bars, Hard Dog roll-over bars

SUMMIT RACING EQUIPMENT
Tel. 216 630 0200
Aftermarket.

TEAM FLATSPOT
15225 S. Foxtail Lane, Phoenix, AZ 85048-9594
Tel. 480-704-5128

TEAM MIATA
1521 Ridgewood Dr. Martinez, CA 94553
Website: www.teammiata.com
Parts and accessories.

TEAM VOODOO
11219 Morning Creek Drive, South San Diego,
CA 92128
Tel. 858-486-4711
Gearknobs, brake handles.

TECHNOSPORTS
34005 Autry, Livonia, MI 48150
Tel. 800-521-4704 and 313 261 0060

TIRE RACK
771 West Chippewa Avenue, South Bend,
IN 46614-3729
Tel. 800-428-8355 and 219-287-2345
Fax 219-236-7707
Aftermarket tyres and wheels.

TODA RACING
AKH Trading, 200 Technology Dr, Suite F, Irvine,
CA 92618
Tel. 949-450-1056
Fax 949-450-1059
Aftermarket.

TRUSSVILLE, MAZDA (FORMERLY ROEBUCK
MAZDA)
Tel. 800-633-8285
Fax 205-886-0195
Dealership and aftermarket.

VIZZON.COM
5153 S. Tabor Way, Littleton, CO 80127-6240
Tel. 303-583-5040
Accessories.

WEAPONR
480 Collins Ave #C, Colma, CA 94015
Tel. 650-992-9669

WESTCO BATTERY
1645 Sinclair street, Anaheim, Ca 92806
Tel. 714-938-5080
Fax 714-938-5307
Replacement batteries.

WHEEL ALIGNMENTS PLUS
174 Terrace Avenue Port Chester, NY 10573
Tel. 914 939 7888

THE WHEEL MACHINE
Website: www.eunos.com/keith/wheels
Keith Tanner's site lets you see how different
wheels would look on your car. (Wheels provided
by The Tire Rack, see above.)

WOLF ACCESSORIES LIMITED
Omega House Sarbir Industrial Park, Cambridge
Road, Harlow, Essex, CM20 2EU
Tel. 01279 411014
Fax 01279 450352
E-mail: sales@wolfmiata.com

Index

European studio, Frankfurt 10,
    48–49, 62–63, 69
Mark One Concept 48–49
Hiroshama HQ/test track 13, 118
R&D budget 10
Tokyo studio, Hiroshima (MC) 12,
    15, 17, 30, 48, 52, 55, 62
Theme A 52, 54–55
Yokohama office 51–52
Mazda Miata Performance Handbook
    11
Mazda engines 27, 47, 53, 58–59, 63,
    67, 71, 75, 79, 108, 136, 140
Familia 1.8 139
Monster 59
Type BE-2E (RS) 60
Type BP-2E (RS) 58
Type B6-ZE 26
Mazda models (incl Limited editions
    and Specials)
Mazda6 69
MBA 99
MX-02 19
MX-03 16
MX-04 Coupé 19
MX-5 Miata
    Mk1 26–27, 30, 47–48, 51, 57–58,
        71, 74–75, 77–80, 90, 94, 114, 129,
        131–133, 135–136, 142, 144–146
    Mk2 29, 47–48, 50–51, 53, 56, 58,
        60–61, 75, 78–80, 91, 99, 106, 129,
        134–136, 142
    'Mk2.5' 62–63, 79
    Mk3 64, 66–70, 79, 94, 102–103,
        108, 129, 131, 135
Arizona 95
BBR Turbo 32, 37, 39, 42, 67, 70,
    82–83
Berkeley 82, 90–91
Black Miata 96
Black SE 76, 86, 96
BRG 82, 96
British Racing Green (1991 SE)
    82–84, 95
California 47, 82, 86–87, 101, 114
California Mk2 92–94, 130
Challenge racers 42
Classic Black 79, 89–90
Dakar 89
Divine 92–94
Gleneagles 47, 79, 82, 86–87
Harvard 79, 90
Icon 94
Isola 92–94
Jasper Conran 82, 92
Laguna Blue and Tan 96
Le Mans 38, 82, 84–85, 123, 132,
    138
M Coupé 44, 47, 49, 51, 53, 55, 57
M edition 82, 96–97

M Speedster 44, 47, 49, 53, 55, 57,
    59, 133–135
M2s 42, 44–45, 108–109
Mahogony mica 98
Merlot 47, 82, 88–89, 101
Miata Detroit 64
Monaco 47, 87, 89
Monza 89
MPS Concept 64, 70, 114
Phoenix 69, 94–95
PS 70
SP 38, 67
Sport 1.8/1.8i 66, 68, 91
STO 97
Sunburst Yellow 96
'Trunk Model' 49–53, 55–57
10th Anniversary 60, 76, 91–92,
    97–98
2001 SE (USA) 98
2002 SE (USA) 98
1.6 42–43, 46, 58, 69, 78–79, 83, 86,
    95, 106, 124, 136, 140
1.6i 86, 89, 94–95
1.8 42–43, 46, 58, 60–61, 63, 69, 79,
    86, 89, 95, 106, 124, 136, 140
1.8i 43, 46, 68, 75, 77, 86, 89–91
1.8iS 43, 46, 91–92
RX-7 10–12, 20, 30, 39, 44, 51, 59,
    67, 69–70, 112
RX-7 R1 141
RX-8 63–64
V705 14, 16–18, 60
Xedos 6
323 10, 16, 26, 36, 39
323F GT 43
323 GTX 136, 139–140
323 MPS (MP3) 64
626 10, 39, 69
929 10, 16
Mazda Australia 64, 67
Mazda Automotive North America 10,
    112
Mazda Motor Italia Spa 127
Mazda Sport Cup 125–126
Mazda UK 103
Mazdaspeed 124
    787B 84
Maztek 73, 89, 132, 138
McCarthy, Mike 35
McCormack, Jonathan 124
McCreath, Martin 18
MCL (Mazda Cars Ltd) 34, 37–38, 40,
    41, 47,67– 68, 70, 82, 84, 90, 92,
    113–114, 124, 142
McLaren F1 supercar 32
McSean, Peter 47
Mercedes 10
Mercury Capri 8
MG 7, 10–11
    MGA 18, 24

MGB 8, 49
MGB GT 8, 53
MGF 7–9, 13, 47, 58–59, 62, 127
MGF Trophy 68
Midget 20, 41, 122
TF 32, 62, 68
Miata Magazine 20, 111–113
Miata (Owner's) Club 11, 110–112,
    142
Miatas at Monterey Festival 112
Michelin tyres 142
Michinori, Yamanouchi 19
Miles, John 32
Miles, Ken 140
Millen, Rod 39
Mini 51, 70
Mini Metro 8
Minilite wheels 26, 77, 142–143
Mitchell, Bill 10
Miyata bicycle 23
Modern Motor magazine 39
Momo steering wheel 89–90,
    106–109
Monster Motorsports 141
    Mega-Monster 141
    Monster Miata 141
Monterey Historic Races 47, 49
Morgan 127
Monza 82, 89–90, 125, 126
Moss 129, 135–138, 142, 146
Motor Sport magazine 84
Mount Panorama track 127
MPV 'kei' car project 12, 16, 19, 27
MSA regulations 124
Mugelli, Massimiliano 126
MX-5 Club New Zealand 99

Nadin, Doug & Charlotte 82, 85, 130,
    138
Nardi steering wheel 55, 58, 92,
    95–97, 106, 107–108
NASA (National Auto Sports Assn)
    123
NEC *Classic and Sportscar* Show 114
New South Wales State Supersprint
    Championship 117, 127
New York Auto Show 53
Newman, Paul 121
Nissan 29
    engine 8
    300ZX 8
nitrous injection 141
Noh masks 30–31
number plate 102, 104–105

Olympic Games, Atlanta 1996 87
One-Make Challenge 39, 41,
    124–125
Open Track Challenge 121
Opel 10

options packages
  A 95
  B 95
  C 95–96
  R 95–96
  Leather 95
  Popular equipment 95, 97
  Power steering 95
Oran Park, Sydney 127
Ostlethwaite, Arnold 'Ginger' 48
owners' clubs (see also Miata Club)
    62, 68, 71–72, 110–118
  Australia 117
  Belgian 114
  Japan 17
  New South Wales 115, 127–128
  New Zealand 99, 114, 141
  South Australia 116
  UK 68, 84, 89, 91, 100, 102, 113,
    115, 124, 129, 145–146

paintwork 74, 78, 145
Panache 141
Panasport wheels 26, 39
Parry-Jones, Richard 69
Pebble Beach Concours 11, 112
Performance Car magazine 39, 61
Peugeot 125
  206 CC 68
Pike's Peak hillclimb 39
Pininfarina 10
Pirelli tyres 90, 108
Pontiac Fiero 17
pop-up headlamps 15, 28–30, 32, 41,
    48, 51–52, 56–57, 74, 78–79, 133
Porsche 10, 29, 64
  Boxster 70
  356 Speedster 48, 59
  911 19, 52, 55, 70, 141
  928 24
  944 20
press reaction 31, 46, 61
Pro Racing Speed World Challenge
    122
Prodrive 67
Production Car Racing Assn of
    Australia 117, 127

racing 26, 41–42, 59, 99, 110–112,
    114, 117, 119–127, 139
Racing Beat 138, 140
Rahal, Bobby 121
Reliant Scimitar 8, 17
Renault
  Mégane Scenic 16
  Speeder 59
  5 Turbo 2 15
Road & Track magazine 17, 35, 61, 64
Roadster Club of Japan 117
Robinson, Tim 113

Robson, Anthony 127
Rod Millen Motorsport 36, 39,
    138–139
roll-over (style) bars 45, 131, 135, 141
Rolls-Royce 92
Rover (see also MG) 13
running costs 71

Sato, Yoichi 12, 15
Saward, Ken 51
SCCA 112, 119–123
scuff plates – see kickplates
Sebring Superchargers 46
Serrano Creek Ranch 22
servicing 100, 105, 144–146
'shaken' inspection 99, 101
Sharp, Scott 121
Shelby, Carroll 132, 140
Shelby Cobra stripes 112, 127,
    132–133
shock absorbers/damping 24, 37,
    42–43, 58–59, 66, 95–96, 102, 106,
    124, 126, 132, 142–143, 145
Shute, John 14, 17
Silverstone 125
Simanaitis, Dennis 35
Southern, Clive 82, 84, 86, 110, 123,
    132, 138
spare wheel 53, 56, 66, 77, 80, 131
spoilers 106, 134–135
Stahl, Michael 46
steering 28, 48, 58, 70, 77, 84, 90, 92,
    95, 106–107, 122
steering wheels 46, 58–59, 86–87,
    89–90, 92, 94–96, 98–99, 102,
    106–107, 129
Stevens, Peter 32, 62
Stewart F1 team 84
Stokes, Donald 7–8
style bars – see roll-over bars
subframe 24, 42–43
Sunbeam Alpine/Tiger 140
supercharging 46, 59, 89, 133,
    137–140
suspension 15, 25–26, 35, 40, 43–44,
    48, 57–59, 61, 64, 66, 68, 77, 96,
    99–100, 124, 136, 142
Sutcliffe, Steve 68
Suzuki 19
  Cappucino 117

Tachibana, Hirotaka 30, 42
Tajima, Mr 31
Tanaka, Shunji 30–31
Tanner, Keith 129, 133, 138
Tickford 70
Tidwell, Vince 111–112
Tokyo Motor Show 16, 19, 57, 61
Top Gear magazine 61
Torque Class magazine 35

Touring Cars 122, 124–125
Toyota 29, 60
  Celica 121
  MR2 13, 15, 17, 29, 48, 68, 99, 127
  Soarer engine 141
transmission 26, 98, 143, 146
  automatic 60, 79, 96–97, 101, 103,
    106, 108–109
treadplates – see kickplates
Trethewey, Roger 116
Triumph 7
  GT6 8, 53
  TR6 8
  TR7 8
Turbo Technics 37
tuning 136–138
turbocharging 37–38, 39, 42, 67, 70,
    82, 137–140
TVR 8, 141
TWR (Tom Walkinshaw Racing) 14,
    37, 75
tyres 26, 42, 56, 60, 64, 77, 96–97,
    105, 142–144

V6 engines 64
V8 engines 140–141
Valvoline Run-off 121–122
van Kelst, Ronald 114
Vassar, Jimmy 121
Vauxhall Nova 124
Vivian, David 61
Vogel, Lyn 'Sky' 112
Volkswagen Beetle 51, 70
Volvo 111

Wankel rotary engine 11, 20, 27, 64,
    112
Warhol, Andy 92
warranty 38, 67, 70, 72, 77, 104
Watanabe, Masaaki 23
Watts, Patrick 124–125
websites 71, 99, 102, 105, 111–112,
    114, 117, 121–122, 124, 127, 129,
    133, 136, 141, 151–152
Wee, Paul 35
weight distribution 25–26, 28, 56
Westfield 124
What Car? magazine 68, 72
What Car? History Check 73
Wheels magazine 35, 46
Whitney, Stan 121
windblocker/windstop 28, 61, 131
wire wheels 142
Wolfson, Dr Phil 112

Yagi, Matsao 10, 14
Yamaguchi, Jack K. 31, 48
Yamamoto, Kenichi 9, 11–12, 19
Yamanouchi, Michinori 12
Yokohama tyres 94, 105, 142